Buildupzion.org/radio
Ibanews.org
N. Sergent 407-489-5679

Hebraic Roots

Ken Garrison

Second printing 2007

Published by Tzemach Institute for Biblical Studies, P.O. Box 181191, Casselberry, Florida 32718. Website: http://www.tzemach.org Email: tzemach@tzemach.org
Questions to the author may be sent to the mailing address above or via email at: ken@tzemach.org

ISBN 0-9669174-0-5
Library of Congress Catalog Card Number: 98-96867

References from the Early Church Fathers were taken from *"Ante-Nicene Fathers"* published by Hendrickson Publishers.

Table of Contents

Part Two: Establishing Hebraic Roots in the Local Church

ACKNOWLEDGMENTS

"Hebraic roots" have been discovered and realized in the experience of the Fellowship Church where I have served as pastor for the past 21 years. I would like to thank the congregation who has been bold in spirit and strong in faith to venture forth in this discovery process. In addition, I would like to express thanks to the many individuals who contributed directly to the preparation of this work: Jon Klein, Larry Dorcik and Pam Cook for their work in reviewing and proofreading the text; Dr. Irving Teitelbaum for his review of the text from a Jewish perspective; Lee Underwood for formatting the text; and Gloria Marxvach for the cover design. Finally, I would like to thank my wife, Jo, for her perseverance while experiencing much of the basis for this work alongside myself and for her encouragement in the long process of writing this text.

Ken Garrison 1998

INTRODUCTION

Often I think about what it would have been like to have been one of Jesus' disciples. What would it have been like to have been taught and discipled directly by the Master, Himself? In a similar way, my mind often considers what it would have been like to have been a part of the early Church in Jerusalem. How clearly the precepts of the Kingdom of God must have been declared by Peter, John and the other disciples. They were Spirit-filled believers; they had been taught directly by Jesus, Himself, and they were ministering in the midst of the people of Israel in Jerusalem. Obviously, this early Church was fully integrated into the fabric of Israel. They embraced all of the prophetic destiny of the people of Israel. They were even seen, and saw themselves, as a sect or denomination of Judaism.

How distant the Christian Church of today appears from that simple beginning. My experience, as a pastor, leads me to think of the divide between the Church and Israel as almost too great to attempt to bridge. Yet the Holy Spirit has repeatedly given powerful witness that this is God's will for us today. Indeed, we represent the first generation since Peter, John and Paul which has the opportunity to discover its roots in Israel and realize these roots in a practical way.

Hebraic Roots was written to outline the path to establish the true Biblical roots of our faith. The information contained herein is readlly documented historically. The conclusions drawn are not based on obscure interpretations of the Scriptures or of history. They flow quite readily from the simple information available to us. The steps outlined have been tested in a local church setting and have been found to provide a great opportunity of witness both in the Jewish and Gentile communities. In other words, the steps outlined here work.

We live in a new age of opportunity in the world. Prior to the regathering of Israel, God's focus of ministry was toward the nations. The Church reached out with the ministry of reconciliation to whomever called on the name of the Lord. Now that Jerusalem is under the authority of a sovereign Jewish state, we have entered a new age. We have opportunities available to us today that no prior generation has had. The message of world deliverance by the hand of God is now appropriate. The establishment of God's literal Kingdom in Jerusalem is at hand. Now, in addition to the message of individual reconciliation to God, we can boldly proclaim God's Kingdom. To be effective in doing this we must be established on a solid Biblical foundation.

The Bible is the only remnant of God's authority left to us. For us to have an effective witness, our faith must be Biblically consistent. Therefore, we must establish Hebraic or Biblical roots in our faith. It is my hope that you will prayerfully read and implement the steps outlined in this book and that the Lord will bring a fresh and bold anointing in His Church through you in this day.

Kenneth E. Garrison
Pastor, Fellowship Church
Casselberry, Florida

Part One:

Hebraic Roots - A Background

1. REDEMPTION AND GOD'S PEOPLE

In order to understand the need for "Hebraic roots", we must understand the overall redemptive plan of God and how He is accomplishing His plan. One of the simplest ways of looking at the problem of man is by considering the subject of authority. When man fell in the Garden, he became his own individual point of authority. Today, there are literally billions of points of authority in the world. Each person struggles with a continuing series of questions to resolve, and each is resolved relative to his own self-interest. Every individual then is pitted against every other for survival.

God is moving to establish a single authority instead. Before the fall, man functioned under the singular authority of God. God's redemptive activity has been aimed at reestablishing His singular authority. Throughout the ages God has been working in different ways to accomplish this goal, but these efforts have always been directly related to this goal. Zechariah prophesied that in the end:

> "And the Lord will be king over all the earth; in that day the Lord will be the only one, and His name the only one".[1]

Paul drew the same conclusion when he stated:

> "And when all things are subjected to Him, then the Son Himself also will be subjected to the One who subjected all things to Him, that God may be all in all".[2]

So when we consider what God is doing, we must do so in light of His overall redemptive purpose.

---

[1]Zechariah 14:9
[2]I Corinthians 15:28

Reference

In the original creation man existed directly under God's authority. Indeed, he was created to serve as the link between God and His creation. We get a glimpse of this arrangement in Psalms 8:

> "O Lord, our Lord, how majestic is Thy name in all the earth, Who hast displayed Thy splendor above the heavens! When I consider Thy heavens, the work of Thy fingers, the moon and the stars, which Thou hast ordained; what is man, that Thou dost take thought of him? And the son of man, that Thou dost care for him. Yet Thou hast made him a little lower than God, and dost crown him with glory and majesty! Thou dost make him to rule over the works of Thy hands; Thou hast put all things under his feet, all sheep and oxen, and also the beasts of the field, the birds of the heavens, and the fish of the sea, whatever passes through the paths of the seas. O Lord, our Lord, how majestic is Thy name in all the earth"![3]

For man to function effectively in this position, he was required to submit to the authority of God. He perceived every thing and every event relative to the person and purpose of God. Each situation was judged "good" or "evil" relative to this perspective.

Two trees are described in the Genesis account: (a) the "Tree of Life" and (b) the "Tree of the Knowledge of Good and Evil". Both trees denote communion or communication: The "Tree of Life" denotes communion with God, and the "Tree of the Knowledge of Good and Evil" denotes communion with Satan. Man originally lived in open communion with God. He submitted to God's authority. He functioned in the capacity for

---

[3]Psalms 8:1,3-9

which God had designed him to function. He saw everything to be "good" or "evil" relative to God. He ate of the "Tree of Life".

We are told that God commanded man not to eat of the "Tree of the Knowledge of Good and Evil". He cautioned man that in the day that he ate of this tree, he would die. Eventually, man did choose to eat of this tree. The Bible gives us no hint as to the period of time that man existed in the garden prior to this event. Since man stood in the direct presence of God having intimate communion with Him, he was continuously renewed. Therefore we would conclude that he lived in a perpetual state.

When man did eat of the "Tree of the Knowledge of Good and Evil", two things occurred which are described in the Genesis account. First, man was driven out from the presence of God. This constitutes spiritual death and would ultimately lead to physical death. The second thing that changed was that man, for the first time, perceived all things and every event "good" or "evil" relative to himself. He saw himself naked and he was afraid. When God encountered man in this condition, He asked,

> "Who told you that you were naked?"[4]

God recognized that man had initiated a line of communication with the one that the Bible calls "the accuser of the brethren",[5] otherwise known as The Satan. Man initiated this line of communication which now would dominate every aspect of his being. He would receive a continual appraisal of every situation judging them as "good" or "evil" relative to himself, becoming the center of his own private little world. He would struggle for what he perceived to be scarce resources in order to provide for himself. Obviously, he would have to compete with every other person for these same resources. Without the blessing and wisdom of God at his disposal, these

---

[4]Genesis 3:11a
[5]Revelation 12:10

resources would be depleted. His capacity to compete would be diminished with age, ultimately leading to death. This sequence of the death process is referred to as the "curse".

This then is the condition that all subsequent generations have been born into. Because it is all man has ever experienced, he considers it natural and normal. He has lost sight of the role for which he was created. This lofty station seems like a fairy tale as he continues to struggle for survival all of his days. Even though man may from time to time acknowledge some responsibility for the stewardship of the earth and the creation, he is always compelled to struggle for his own private survival.

Only an intervention from outside of mankind could significantly change the situation. Man is hopeless on his own. We maintain that such an intervention is in process. We call that process "redemption". The account of "redemption" is recorded in the Bible. God, from the time that man was driven out from His presence, has been patiently working to bring all things back into order, i.e., under His authority again. Since, by God's own design in creation, man was created to serve as His authority figure in the world, man must be the one brought into submission to God.

Therefore, when we consider what God is doing, we must do so in light of His overall redemptive purpose, because all He does is consistent with this purpose. So if we study His covenants, we must do so in light of His purpose of establishing His singular authority in the universe. If we consider the subject of individual salvation, we must do so again in the same light.

Covenants and Election

We now will consider the concept of covenant. In modern legal terminology, a covenant is a contract. We make many contracts throughout our lifetime. A contract is simply an agreement between two or more parties which defines the purpose and conditions of that relationship. A Biblical covenant does the same thing. In the Scriptures we can clearly see three covenants that God has made as a part of His redemptive plan. These are the (1) *Abrahamic Covenant*, (2) the *Mosaic Covenant*, and the (3) *Ben-Davidic* (son of David) *Covenant*. In each case God chose the party He would enter into covenant with, He revealed Himself to the one chosen, and He specified the terms and conditions of the covenant. The covenant partners either accepted or rejected the covenant.

The covenant partners of God are designated as the "elect". Election means simply that a person or persons have been specifically selected to enter into covenant relationship with God. God always chooses those who are to become His covenant partners. Therefore, we may say that the one elected *never* chooses himself, but is chosen by God. A natural conclusion that we must draw from considering this process is that it is not "fair" when considered purely on humanistic grounds. Therefore, we say that God exercises His sovereignty in the election. We also conclude that not all human beings are elect in terms of God's covenants.

Election and Salvation

Most people believe intuitively that God is "fair". As a result they feel awkward with the concept of election. Often there are attempts to relate the concept of election with the concept of salvation (being saved from eternal separation from God). In order to be "fair", doctrines are developed that indicate that the election of God is now universal, i.e., everyone is "elect". In fact, election is not related to salvation. God chooses people to become His vessel in the world to work out His purpose of establishing a single authority in the universe. Those elect have a unique opportunity to become "co-workers" with God but this does not guarantee their individual salvation. Those not elect in accordance with the covenants, nevertheless, have the option of salvation. Indeed

Peter boldly proclaimed that God is patient:

> "not wishing for any to perish but for all to come to repentance".[6]

Paul declared that God:

> "desires all men to be saved and to come to the knowledge of the truth".[7]

We, therefore, conclude that the concept of election and the concept of salvation are not related. One may be elect and not saved. On the other hand, one may be saved and not elect.

---

[6] II Peter 3:9b
[7] I Timothy 2:4

2. TWO COVENANTS - TWO PEOPLES

Israel and the Church have legitimate covenants and complementary roles in God's purpose in the earth. The respective covenants stem from the Abrahamic covenant and together encompass those elect in the world; those through whom God has chosen to accomplish His purpose. The original covenant was made by God with Abraham. This covenant was later confirmed to his son, Isaac, and his grandson, Jacob. In this covenant God initiated the redemptive process that He intended to carry out in the world. While promising a number of blessings to Abraham, God revealed His redemptive aims by saying that through Abraham, God would bless all the families of the earth:

> "And in you all the families of the earth shall be blessed".[1]

Most of the provisions of the Abrahamic covenant were confirmed by God when He established His covenant with Israel at Mt. Sinai. God promised to make Israel a "nation of priests"[2]. He would set Israel,

> "high above all nations which He has made, for praise, fame and honor".[3]

God would give to Israel the land that He had promised to Abraham, Isaac and Jacob.[4] And God would continue the redemptive process through this elect vessel, the nation of Israel.

Later (around 1000 BC) God made a covenant with King David who served as a type of the coming Messiah. God promised David that his son would stand in a very special position of anointing:

---

[1]Genesis 12:3b
[2]Exodus 19:6
[3]Deuteronomy 26:19
[4]Exodus 23:31

> "When your days are complete and you lie down with your fathers, I will raise up your descendant after you, who will come forth from you, and I will establish his kingdom. He shall build a house for My name, and I will establish the throne of his kingdom forever".[5]

These covenants that God made with Israel and with David stem from the original covenant made with Abraham. Each represents God's choice of an individual or a people to serve Him as He pursues the redemptive process. We will investigate some aspects of the covenants that God has made.

In order to set the stage for discussing the covenants, there are four basic premises that need to be stated:

> (1) Subsequent to the Abrahamic Covenant, God has established two basic covenants as recorded in the Scriptures: One with Israel through Moses at Mt. Sinai and the other with followers of Jesus. The latter covenant was initially stated to David[6] and made with the "*Ben-David*", Solomon. It is being fulfilled through Jesus.
>
> (2) Individually a person can relate to God through only one covenant at a given time.
>
> (3) There has developed, therefore, two great peoples; one associated with each covenant.
>
> (4) God intends for these two peoples to complement one another to affect His purpose of redemption. Each functions

---

[5]II Samuel 7:12-13

[6]II Samuel 7:8-16

differently but shares a common identity.

With these basic premises we now consider the nature of these covenants. The characteristics of each are outlined in Table 1. Note some of the dissimilarities between these covenants. The focus of the Mosaic covenant has always been centered around the nation of people in the land of Israel. The focus of the Ben-Davidic covenant has always been on the King. Throughout the centuries the Jewish people have looked persistently to the day of their regathering to the land of Israel. We hear this in the Passover Seder which is closed with the prayer "*L'Shannah Haba'ah B'Yerushalim*" meaning "may we celebrate this festival next year in Jerusalem". In contrast, the Church has never exhibited much concern for the Land. Its concern is for serving the King and ultimately being gathered to Him.

The message or ministry of Israel is different from that of the Church. When the people of Israel are living in their land, they become a nation under God's specific authority and are to be witnesses to all other nations relative to the blessing secured by serving God. While dispersed, Israel brings a warning of God's judgment to all other nations.[7] When Israel is in the Land the message of the Church is "The Kingdom of God". When Israel is dispersed, the Church bears a twofold ministry: (1) to comfort and encourage Israel[8] and (2) to preach to the Gentiles the message of personal reconciliation to God.[9] Basically, in the diaspora, Israel gives testimony that God will shake or destroy the nations (national units), while the Church extends the hope of salvation to the individuals of those nations. Over the centuries both groups have largely lost track of their original message and function. Each has adopted a basic mentality of survival in the dispersion.

---

[7]Jeremiah 25:15-29
[8]Isaiah 40:1-2 and Romans 15:8
[9]II Corinthians 5:18

There are some questions which always arise when we speak of Israel existing in a valid and active covenant with God. Do we conclude that all Jews are saved? Expressed in another way, will all Jews live eternally with God after physical death, if we say that Israel's covenant is valid and active? The answer is no! Israel's covenant is a national covenant, i.e., God uses Israel as a nation. Individual Jews, like individual Gentiles, will have to stand before God and give an account for their lives upon parting this present life.[10] Judgment is always in the hands of God and we must leave it there. It is sufficient to say that,

> "it is appointed for men to die once and after this comes judgment".[11]

Each of us, whether from Jewish or Gentile backgrounds, are directly accountable unto God in judgment.

Another question that often arises is focused on the concept that Israel's covenant has become obsolete according to the statements recorded in Hebrews 8:7 and 8:13.

> "For if that first covenant had been faultless, there would have been no occasion sought for a second".[12]

And,

> "When He said, "A new covenant," He has made the first obsolete. But whatever is becoming obsolete and growing old is ready to disappear".[13]

At first reading, this would appear to be the case. However, if so interpreted, this Scripture would be in direct conflict with other Scriptures which indicate that God's covenant with Israel is eternal.[14] Since all other Scriptures indicate the eternal nature of God's covenant with Israel, such interpretation would

---

[10]Malachi 3:16-18
[11]Hebrews 9:27
[12]Hebrews 8:7
[13]Hebrews 8:13
[14]Genesis 17:7, Jeremiah 31:35-37 and Romans 11:25-29

render this portion and, hence, the book of Hebrews as unscriptural. Realizing this, we must consider other interpretations of Hebrews 8:7 and 8:13.

Since the book of Hebrews was written to individual believers from Jewish backgrounds, hence the name Hebrews, and since these believers were evidently considering a return to Judaism; we conclude that the exhortation relative to the "old" covenant is applicable only in their own individual lives. Therefore, for them as individuals, the first covenant (their lives as Israelites before personally receiving the revelation of Messiah Jesus) has gone out of existence as they became individually a part of the new. Remember one of our basic premises: one can be an active participant in only one covenant at a given time. What we must not conclude is that the covenant itself is going out of existence in a general sense. In other words, we must *not* interpret Hebrews 8 as indicating that God has abrogated His covenant with the nation of Israel. This is precisely what the Church fathers of the second, third, and fourth centuries *did conclude*. This has, in turn, provided the basis for the concept that the Church has now replaced Israel.

We conclude therefore that God has two major active covenants to accomplish His purpose in the earth. Each covenant has a great people who have been joined to God by the covenant. We must always remember that existing in one of God's covenants does not mean that we are special of ourselves, or that God loves us or is concerned about us more than for any other people. Each covenant represents a unique opportunity for righteousness in God's purpose. The true outworking of either covenant should complement the other in order for God's purpose to advance.

With this understanding firmly in mind, we are to rejoice in our calling and open ourselves to becoming more fruitful vessels for the outworking of His purpose. As believers in Messiah Jesus we have a special opportunity relative to Israel and, likewise, Israel today has a unique opportunity relative to the Church. Today is the day of great opportunities. Men and women of true faith must realize this and act on it.

Table 1. God's Redemptive Covenants

Covenant/Traits	People	Purpose	Ultimate Goal
Mosaic	Israel	*In the land of Israel:*	To return to the land and live
Land		Serve as a model nation.	there under God's authority.
Circumcision		*In the dispersion:*	
Law		Announce judgment to the nations.	
Ben-Davidic	Church	*With Israel in the land:*	To be gathered to the King.
House		Preach the Kingdom of God.	
Throne		*With Israel in the dispersion:*	
Kingdom		Preach reconciliation to the nations. Encourage Israel.	

3. SEPARATION OF THE CHURCH FROM ISRAEL

Today when we consider the Church and Israel we see two totally independent entities. It is evident to those of us who have embraced a vision of establishing churches with Hebraic roots, that both the Church and Synagogue are content with the separation. In fact, any suggestion of change makes both groups very uncomfortable. We want to investigate (1) how this separation took place and (2) who is responsible for it. Finally, we would like to (3) establish a Biblical vision of mutual cooperation which we believe God originally intended.

The first church was established in Jerusalem. It was made up exclusively of people from Jewish backgrounds. We believe from our study of the book of Acts that they were observant Jews in every sense of the word. They evidently worshiped in the Temple,

> "Now Peter and John were going up to the temple at the ninth hour, the hour of prayer".[1]

They studied in the synagogues,

> "But going on from Perga, they arrived at Pisidian Antioch, and on the Sabbath day they went into the synagogue and sat down".[2]

They obviously participated in everyday Jewish life. Nevertheless, they were different. They each had experienced God's Holy Spirit bringing them into His presence. They enjoyed this awesome sense of communion with God. Notable miracles occurred through them. They became distinguished as the sect called "*The Way*".[3] "The Way" implied the way of direct communion with God. Messiah Jesus declared that He was,

> "the way, and the truth, and the life; no one

---

[1]Acts 3:1
[2]Acts 13:14
[3]Acts 9:2

> comes to the Father, but through Me".[4]

The early Church was experiencing this awesome communion with God in Messiah Jesus.

We conclude that the earliest Jerusalem church existed in the midst of the greater community of Israel but were separated from it by a unique God-given anointing. God by His own choice had distinguished or separated the Church from Israel. The Church continued in this situation for a period of two to ten years. During this time there were conflicts between the Church leaders and the leaders of other sects, but this type of opposition was typical of that experienced between the various sects.

The second major step taken by God to further separate the Church from Israel occurred in Caesarea.[5] A Gentile centurion by the name of Cornelius was told in a vision to send for Peter. God expressly intervened by revelation to Peter convincing him to go to the home of Cornelius. Peter went and while he preached concerning Jesus, the household of Cornelius boldly received the same anointing that the Jewish believers had received on "*Yom Hashavuot*" (Day of Pentecost).

> "While Peter was still speaking these words, the Holy Spirit fell upon all those who were listening to the message. And all the circumcised believers who had come with Peter were amazed, because the gift of the Holy Spirit had been poured out upon the Gentiles also. For they were hearing them speaking with tongues and exalting God".[6]

Those present from Jewish backgrounds were amazed that God had poured out this distinctive anointing upon these Gentiles. Peter, on the basis of what he saw God doing,

---

[4]John 14:6
[5]Acts 10
[6]Acts 10:44-46a

openly received them into fellowship. He immediately baptized them. This step was very momentous because these Gentiles were openly received within the fellowship without the customary steps of conversion that were required by the Scriptures for Gentiles to be accepted within Israel. As a result, a great conflict was initiated.

After these things, the Church began to be spread throughout the dispersion. Paul made numerous missionary journeys throughout the Roman Empire and was very fruitful in establishing churches in many Gentile cities. Much of our New Testament is made up of letters from Paul to these newly-established churches. During this era the Church continued to see itself and to be seen as a part of Israel, i.e., a sect of Judaism, although the distinction between Israel and the Church was evident to all.

We conclude that God sovereignly chose to distinguish the Church from Israel. Israel was already sanctified from the nations by God's covenant with them. The Church was even further sanctified or distinguished from Israel by His anointing. Later we will develop the argument that God did this to provide a vessel of anointing within Israel which would complement His outworking through Israel. We do not believe God intended to initiate a totally separate group unrelated to Israel in function and identity.

World events also began to play a significant role in further separating the Church from Israel. Israel had been under Roman domination since the time of Pompeii (64 BC). Many in Israel were desperate to overthrow Roman dominance in order to establish an independent Jewish State. In 66 AD the Zealots gained an upper hand and war broke out.[7] Eventually Roman armies surrounded Jerusalem exactly fulfilling the prophecies spoken forty years earlier by Jesus,

> "But when you see Jerusalem surrounded by armies, then recognize that her desolation is at

[7]Marvin Wilson, *Our Father Abraham*, Grand Rapids and Dayton, 1989, pg. 75

> hand. Then let those who are in Judea flee to the mountains, and let those who are in the midst of the city depart, and let not those who are in the country enter the city; because these are days of vengeance, in order that all things which are written may be fulfilled".[8]

Jesus instructed His followers to flee in such an event and they did so. The general community of Israel saw them as traitors. Titus destroyed Jerusalem and the Temple. He killed or took captive multitudes from Jerusalem and Judea. The open conflict between Rome and Israel continued for the next sixty-five years until the final humiliation of Israel by Hadrian as he harshly put down the "Bar Kochba Revolt".

The era from 66 AD until 135 AD was most difficult for both Israel and the Church. Jerusalem and the Temple had been destroyed; that which had provided an important unifying tie between both groups was now lost. Intense persecution of Jews and Christians led both groups to develop a defensive attitude about themselves. The Jewish people could not overlook the fact that the Church had forsaken the revolt against Rome. The Church at the same time began to discover that it was advantageous to see itself independent of Israel and began to embrace a universal (catholic or non-national) identity.

As men from Gentile backgrounds came to leadership positions in the Church, the tie with Israel was further weakened. We see in Ignatius' epistle to the Magnesians, written around 110 AD, that the Shabbat was soon ignored and worship was encouraged on the first day of the week.

> "If, therefore, those who were brought up in the ancient order of things have come to the possession of a new hope, no longer observing the shabbat, but living in the observance of the Lord's Day on which also our life has sprung up

---

[8]Luke 21:20-22

> again by Him and by His death - whom some deny...."[9]

This was called the "*Lord's Day*" because the resurrection occurred on this day of the week. The Jewish people were soon seen as having been cut off from God's plan, and the Church began to develop the theological argument that it had replaced Israel and had become the "New Israel". Eventually, the Biblical feasts or festivals were replaced by Christian festivals. Finally, in the time of Constantine, the Church defined its concept of God's being. The vision of God was changed from the Biblical revelation of the Holy One of Israel who had anointed His unique Messiah by His Ruah Hakodesh (Holy Spirit) and subsequently anointed His chosen vessel (the Church) with the same spirit, and was re-defined as the Holy Trinity (three coexistent and coequal manifestations making up the Being of God). Since such a definition was directly contrary to Biblical revelation, this action sealed the separation between the Church and Israel.

With the Temple destroyed, Israel redefined its faith and practice. The oral interpretation of the Law, the *Mishna*, was codified by 200 AD. Over the next several centuries this was supplemented by the *Gemora* to form the *Talmud*. Temple worship was carried over into the synagogue and the home. Israel prepared for survival in the dispersion.

Thus, today, we see these two entities in the world: the Church and the Synagogue. Each denies union with the other; both are comfortable with the separation. However, it seems obvious that God never intended such a separation. According to Paul's exhortation to the Romans, the Church must see itself grafted into the rich olive tree or it will be cut off. He specifically exhorted the Church,

> "Do not be arrogant toward the branches: but if you are arrogant, remember that it is not you who supports the root, but the root supports you.

---

[9]Magnesians 9:8-10

> You will say then, "Branches were broken off so that I might be grafted in." Quite right, they were broken off for their unbelief, but you stand by your faith. Do not be conceited, but fear; for if God did not spare the natural branches, neither will He spare you".[10]

Elsewhere, Paul described believers as being part of "the Commonwealth of Israel".[11] Obviously, God intended the Church to share a common identity with that of Israel. The Church was to be a simple extension of Israel distinguished by God's anointing, but one in identity and ultimate purpose. God never intended two trees. He intended one and that was Israel, rooted in covenant, Torah, land and people, and branched out in anointing with worldwide scope in introducing God's Kingdom into the world. Today, God is calling for the Church to repent from its separate identity, to humble itself, and to acknowledge its ties with Israel, its "Hebraic roots".

---

[10]Romans 11:18-21
[11]Ephesians 2:12

4. THE FURTHER SEPARATION

Why did the Church further the separation of itself from Israel beyond what God had done? To help us understand this, we will consider the story of Jeroboam ben Nebat. The story is recorded in I Kings 12:16-33. God anointed Jeroboam to be king of the Northern Kingdom as a part of the judgment on the house of David due to the sins of Solomon. The judgment occurred during the reign of Rehoboam ben Solomon. Rehoboam reigned only over the tribe of Judah and Benjamin; Jeroboam ruled over the other tribes.

It is obvious from our text that Jeroboam did not trust the Lord to establish the kingdom He had promised him. The Temple remained in Jerusalem, the Altar of the Lord was there and the Levitical priesthood ministered there. Jeroboam was afraid that if the people in his kingdom continued to worship, according to Scripture, in Jerusalem, that soon they would defect to Judah and serve the King of Judah and Jeroboam's kingdom would lose its separate identity. He thought he would lose his throne. In reaction to this, Jeroboam committed three specific sins.

First, he built an idol (two golden calves) and said to Israel,

> "behold your gods, O Israel, that brought you up
> from the land of Egypt".[1]

In other words, he declared to Israel that these idols were really the Biblical God.

Secondly, he built altars before these idols at Bethel and Dan. Sacrifices were offered on these altars rather than on the Altar of the Lord in Jerusalem. This also was a sin because God expressly forbade offerings at any place other

---

[1] I Kings 12:28

than that place where He established His name, i.e., Jerusalem.

> "But you shall seek the Lord at the place which the Lord your God shall choose from all your tribes, to establish His name there for His dwelling, and there you shall come".[2]

Thirdly, Jeroboam instituted a unique festival which rivaled the festivals of the Lord,

> "And Jeroboam instituted a feast in the eighth month on the fifteenth day of the month, like the feast which is in Judah, and he went up to the altar; thus he did in Bethel, sacrificing to the calves which he had made. And he stationed in Bethel the priests of the high places which he had made. Then he went up to the altar which he had made in Bethel on the fifteenth day in the eighth month, even in the month which he had devised in his own heart; and he instituted a feast for the sons of Israel, and went up to the altar to burn incense".[3]

This festival was established in the eighth Hebrew month (Cheshvan, October/November) and appears to have been patterned after the festival of Sukkot. In this manner Jeroboam sealed the separation of the Northern Kingdom from the Southern Kingdom of Judah. Eventually the tribes he led were dispersed by Assyria (722 BC) never to have a national identity again. Remnants of all these tribes have been preserved in the Jewish people;[4] nevertheless, the Kingdom of Israel itself was destroyed forever due to the sin of its first king, Jeroboam. Hosea prophesied that this remnant would be preserved in the Jewish people when he said,

> "Afterward the sons of Israel will return and seek

---

[2]Deuteronomy 12:5
[3]I Kings 12:32-33
[4]II Chronicles 30:1-12

> the Lord their God and David their King, and they will come trembling to the Lord and to His goodness in the last days".[5]

We have considered the sins of Jeroboam because they have been repeated in the Church for exactly the same reasons --- to establish and maintain an identity for the Church separate from Israel. It is obvious that Jesus instructed His disciples in the worship of the God of Abraham, the God of Isaac and the God of Jacob. He specifically quoted the *Shema*,

> "Hear, O Israel! The Lord our God is one Lord".[6]

During the apostolic era the leaders of the Church followed this form of worship. However, in the second and third centuries Christian doctrine evolved beyond Biblical revelation. Finally, at the council of Nicea, convened and directed by Caesar Constantine, Jesus was defined as being of the same essence as the Father.[7] Later, in the General Council held in Constantinople in 381 AD, the Holy Spirit was defined in the same way. These definitions of God were based on philosophical speculation as to His nature, rather than on Biblical revelation because the Bible does not define the detailed relationship of the Father, Jesus and the Holy Spirit. Thus, the basis for the mystical Holy Trinity was formulated by the bishops of the Church. Later, Augustine developed the concept further in his writings. It has become universally accepted in the Church since then. There is some Biblical basis for understanding that God has been manifested as a triune being. We believe that this is obvious from the New Testament literature. We are opposed, however, to the <u>definition</u> of God as the mystical Holy Trinity because this contradicts directly the name of God revealed to Moses,

---

[5] Hosea 3:5
[6] Mark 12:29
[7] Isaac Boyle, *A Historical View of the Council of Nice*, (Baker Book House, Grand Rapids), pg.20

> אֶהְיֶה אֲשֶׁר אֶהְיֶה -- "I Will Be that which I Will Be".[8]

God boldly declared that man could not define Him. This is exactly what the Bishops of the Church did as they defined the Holy Trinity. In this manner, the Church defined for itself a god, the mystical Holy Trinity, not conforming to the simple revelation of Scripture, and labeled this god as the true Biblical God. It would not be wrong to speak of God being revealed in the New Testament era as Father, Son and Holy Spirit. It is wrong to say that this defines God. Thus, the Church followed the sin of Jeroboam and affected exactly the same results --- a determined separation from the Jewish people who held to a Biblical definition and revelation of God.

Jeroboam's sin of erecting alien altars was repeated by the Church as the Altar of God was universalized. This step was aided by the fact that Titus destroyed the Altar of the Lord in 70 AD when he destroyed the Temple in Jerusalem. The sacrifices ceased after this time. The Altar of the Lord, both in the Tabernacle and, later, in the Temple, was seen as the physical counterpart of a Heavenly one,

> "And see that you make them after the pattern for them, which was shown to you on the mountain";[9]

and,

> "who serve a copy and shadow of the heavenly things, just as Moses was warned by God when he was about to erect the tabernacle; for, 'See', He says, 'that you make all things according to the pattern which was shown you on the mountain'";[10]

yet, God declared that the physical altar would be established

---

[8]Exodus 3:14
[9]Exodus 25:40
[10]Hebrews 8:5

forever,

> "For now I have chosen and consecrated this house that My name may be there forever, and My eyes and My heart will be there perpetually".[11]

In the Christian view, the destruction of the physical altar was interpreted as a declaration that it was obsolete to God's purpose. Christians saw the heavenly altar mystically associated with the sanctuary of the Church. Thus, the Altar of God was seen as universal and unconnected with a given geographical location. The Church saw, and continues to see, no need for the Altar of God in Jerusalem due to the concept of a universal spiritual altar. Again, the separation with Israel was effected.

The final sin in which the Church followed the pattern of Jeroboam was in the matter of Biblical festivals. The most important Biblical festival by Jewish reckoning is the weekly Shabbat.[12] God said specifically that this would be a sign between Him and His people,

> "So the sons of Israel shall observe the sabbath, to celebrate the sabbath throughout their generations as a perpetual covenant. It is a sign between Me and the sons of Israel forever; for in six days the Lord made heaven and earth, but on the seventh day He ceased from labor, and was refreshed".[13]

As early as the second century, the Church adopted a Sunday "shabbat" and by doing so denied their union with the Biblical God and His people.

Again, at the time of Constantine, the matter of a weekly festival was considered. In 321 AD, Constantine forbade work

---

[11]II Chronicles 7:16

[12]Samuel T. Lochs and Saul P. Wachs, *Judaism* Argus Communications, Niles, Illinois, pg. 73

[13]Exodus 31:16-17

on Sundays in the cities.[14] Other festivals such as Easter and Christmas were defined separate from Biblical revelation to distinguish Christian practice from Jewish practice. Easter had been separated from the Jewish Passover as early as 200 AD. Christmas was associated with the pagan Roman festival of Sol Invictus and celebrated on the 25th of December. Thus, the Church defined for itself an entire set of festivals which were different from the Biblical festivals. This effectively defined Christians as a separate people from Israel.

The sins of Jeroboam were repeated by the Church. Changes in Christian doctrine and practice evolved throughout the second and third centuries. Constantine, early in the fourth century, locked the changes into Roman Law at the first General Council of the Church at Nicea. Little has changed since that time. Following the guidance of Constantine, the bishops readily laid aside Biblical revelation to establish a religion totally separated from God's people, Israel. That religion has been passed down to our own day. When the reformation occurred, these most basic doctrines were left unquestioned. The reformation Churches carried over these universal concepts into their own practice; they remain as such today.

Now God is calling for repentance. Israel has returned to its land. Jerusalem is under Jewish control. Christians are being challenged to embrace their real roots. Will local churches be grafted into Israel according to Romans 11 or into Universal Christianity? Which way will we go? Repentance must come in three areas:

(1) From the mystical Holy Trinity to the worship of the Holy One of Israel and His Messiah in the Holy Spirit;

(2) From a universal spiritual altar to the

---

[14]Williston Walker, *A History of the Christian Church*, Charles Scribner's Sons, NY, pg. 105

Altar of the Lord in Jerusalem; and

(3) From Sunday Shabbat and Constantinian festivals to Biblical Shabbat and festivals.

That church, or those churches, which cling to the Constantinian tradition will almost certainly become the false prophet envisioned by John,[15] who stands alongside the final "beast" government of the earth. We see bold overtures in the world toward a one-world government. We believe that we are also approaching the manifestation of a representative one-world religion. That one-world "beast" government and religion will ultimately attempt to destroy God's people Israel. As true Biblical believers, we have the opportunity and responsibility to stand in unity of identity and purpose with Israel as this challenge develops.

---

[15]Revelation 13 and 19

5. DOCTRINAL DEVELOPMENT BY THE CHURCH

The Church was established during the first century AD, first by Messiah Jesus in His earthly ministry, then by His disciples. We have the New Testament as a record of these events. During the apostolic era, the apostles and the Jerusalem church provided a central authority for the early Church. With the death of the apostles and the destruction of Jerusalem, that authority was removed. In the second and third centuries, the Church changed markedly due to a number of pressures. There was little unifying central authority during this era. There was considerable Greek philosophical and cultural influence introduced into the Church. Christianity, as it evolved in this era, was considered illegal in the Roman Empire; it experienced persecution from time to time. As a result of these and other pressures, the doctrinal position of Christianity evolved throughout this period. This came to an end with Constantine and the first General Council of the Church at Nicea.

Following the time of Constantine, in the fifth century, Augustine served to codify and define the Church position in such a way that could be easily understood. His interpretation of Church position has been extremely influential. Few significant changes have been made since the time of Augustine. (See Table 2)

Challenges and Reactions

Lack of Central Authority in the Church

During the first Century, the original apostles continued to exert strong influence over the Church. As a result, the Hebraic character of the early Church was maintained relatively faithful to that vision set forth by Messiah Jesus. Obviously, the impact of men like Peter, John and Paul was sufficient to guard the doctrinal positions of the Church and to avoid acceptance of unscriptural positions. Peter and Paul probably died during the seventh decade of the first century. Most maintain that John lived to near the end of the century.

The period from 70 AD to 110 AD has very little documentation that can help us understand what took place. However, after 110 AD, we have recorded literature available from the Church leaders of the second and subsequent centuries. Walker summarizes this era:

> "Yet though some gleanings can be recovered from this period, the forty years from 70 to 110 remain one of the obscurest portions of church history. This is the more to be regretted because they were an epoch of rapid change in the church itself. When the characteristics of the church can once more be clearly traced, its general conception of Christianity shows surprisingly little of the distinctive stamp of Paul. Not only must many now unknown missionaries have labored in addition to the great apostle, but an inrush of ideas from other than Christian sources, brought undoubtedly by converts of heathen antecedents, modified Christian beliefs and practices, especially regarding the sacraments, fasting, and the rise of liturgical forms. The old conviction of the immediacy of the guidance of the Spirit faded, without becoming wholly extinguished".[1]

After about 110 AD, Church literature reflects a considerable shift in position from that maintained in the New Testament writings. The position of the Church continued to evolve through the third century. There was no clear cut authority that governed the Church, therefore, local leaders were relatively free to modify their position without much interference. Most

---

[1]Walker, *A History of the Christian Church*, pgs. 30-31

Table 2. Post Biblical History

Apostolic Age[1]	Transition Era[2]	Evolution of Christianity[3]	Constantinian Church Era[4]

30 AD — 70 AD — 135 AD — 325 AD

1 Apostolic Age - Church seen as a part of Judaism - Period of apostolic authority - Church maintained Hebraic characteristics and roots.

2 Transition Period - After the destruction of the Temple and Jerusalem, there was a 40 year period of great transition. There is little literature from this period to give understanding. The Church appeared completely changed at the end of this period.

3 Christianity evolved as a separate religion - During this period there was an open debate and development of Christian theology. Often this was shaped by philosophy or by the struggle against heresies. Christianity was illegal in the Roman Empire. Persecution of the Church occurred, although, general, widespread persecutions were rare.

4 Christianity and the Empire became intertwined - Constantine used the Church as a grassroots political organization. Christianity was made legal and eventually was made the religion of the empire.

of the leaders of the second and subsequent centuries were from Gentile backgrounds and did not have any strong allegiance to Hebraic interpretation or practice. As a result, pagan influences were readily introduced into church practice evidently without significant objection. The local church competed with the local synagogue and the seeds of competition and mistrust were sown. Neither the Church nor the synagogue have recovered from this mistrust.

Finally, in the fourth century, Constantine reversed the Roman position concerning the Church. He made Christianity, as it had evolved to his day, the official religion of the Roman Empire. Church law and Roman law became intertwined. General Councils of the Church were convened to determine doctrinal positions for the Church. The period of relatively free evolution for the Church was over. A central authority had once again been established; the doctrines of the Church were locked into position. It would be very difficult to change those positions in the future. Even to this day the vast majority of the Christian Church embraces those positions fixed by the early Church councils.

Gnosticism

There were a number of cultic influences that served to mold the Church position as the religion of Christianity was being defined. One of the most influential movements was "Gnosticism". Gnosticism was a syncretistic philosophy adopting concepts from many existing philosophies. It taught a dualistic philosophy characteristic of the Persians. It maintained that the "spiritual" existence was higher than the lower "material" existence. Special knowledge was required to attain to the higher spiritual existence. This was salvation to the Gnostic. The Gnostics taught that Jesus was never born of the flesh (lower material world), but only appeared to have done so. He was seen as revealing the true god of the higher spiritual world as contrasted to the god of the Old Testament who was concerned with the material or lower world. Due to Paul's emphasis on the old and new natures, the Gnostics embraced the writings of Paul as contrasted to the other writers of the New Testament.

Gnosticism flourished during the second century. Its influence threatened early Christianity. Many Church leaders rose to the challenge of confronting Gnosticism. However, as a result of the struggle, many gnostic ideas were incorporated into Christianity. For example, the concept that we have received salvation and will "go to heaven" when we die is a result of gnostic influence. It reflects the concept of evolving or going on to a higher, spiritual existence. In fact, true Biblical revelation shows us that God is preparing to come down to earth and dwell in the midst of man; that a dominant purpose of God's people is to prepare a place for Him, not simply to get ready to go "up" and join Him in heaven.

Another influence of Gnosticism is that the Hebrew Scriptures (Old Testament) are often received as inferior to the Messianic Scriptures (New Testament). Church leaders would deny this, but in reality, little emphasis is given to the Hebrew Scriptures while major emphasis is given to the letters of Paul. This is exactly what the Gnostics did.

Finally, Gnostics emphasized special or secret knowledge that resulted in salvation. Today in the Church we hear terms like, "coming to a saving knowledge of Christ". This is in contrast to the Biblical concept that true believers are elect or chosen by God according to His purpose. Our relationship is based on His call and our response or obedience to Him. We are saved as we interact with the risen savior and the Holy One.[2] Salvation is not a result of some special knowledge.

Rejection by Rome

In the Roman Empire, a religion was considered legitimate if it was more ancient than the Empire[3]. Therefore, Judaism

---

[2]Romans 5:11

[3]Clarence Wagner, *Covenants*, Bridges for Peace, Jerusalem, Israel

was considered as a legitimate religion and, hence, was legal in the empire. During much of the first century, the Church was seen as a sect of Judaism[4] and, therefore, it was seen as legal. During the second century, the Church clearly separated itself from Judaism and defined itself as universal (or catholic). Since it was seen as evolving during the latter part of the first and the early part of the second century, it was seen as a "new" religion and therefore was considered illegal by Rome. Church leaders arose to the challenge of defending the Christian position. These were the "apologists" of the second and third centuries. Often these apologists appealed to Greek philosophy as much as to Biblical truth in presenting their arguments. This provided a back-door entrance of Greek thought into the evolving theology of Christian doctrine.

A related development regarding the defense of Christianity was the effort to show that Christianity was the legitimate continuation of the ancient religion of Israel. If this could be proven, then Christianity would be shown to be legal since it would have existed for millennia. But in order to show that Christianity was the legitimate continuation of the religion of Israel one had to prove that Judaism was the illegitimate continuation of that same religion. Hence the concept of "replacement theology" was introduced by Church leaders. By this means, "replacement theology" became a foundational part of the doctrine of Christianity.

Greek Philosophical Influence

Early Christianity evolved in the geographical regions where Greek philosophy had its strongest base in the ancient world. As a result, the Gentile leaders of the Church were often strongly influenced by Greek thought, perhaps without even realizing it. The effect of Greek thought can, however, be seen. For example, the Greek philosopher Protagoras said, "Man is the measure of all things". This states the

---

[4]Acts 24:14

ultimate premise of humanism. This focus on man became a defining part of Christianity. Messiah Jesus declared that the first and greatest commandment was,

> "And you shall love the Lord your God with all your heart, and with all your soul and with all your mind, and with all your strength".[5]

This is opposite to Greek thought. However, in Christianity, concern for man has far exceeded concern for God. Indeed, concern for the well-being of man (or mankind) is seen as equivalent to concerning ourselves with God. Thus, much of modern Christianity is a haven for humanistic thought and sentiment.

Legal Embrace of Rome

Probably the most deadly influence on Christianity was its eventual acceptance in the Roman Empire. By the time Constantine had become head of the Empire, its stability was being challenged by internal decay and attacks from without. Constantine realized that he needed some entity that could serve as a disciplined backbone which would provide a unifying influence for the Empire. He envisioned using the Church for this purpose. In order to do so, He declared Christianity the official religion of Rome. He restored formerly confiscated property to the Church,[6] and gave bishops government pensions. Above all he projected thc Church into the position of ultimate political acceptance in the community. The acceptance, the power and the wealth totally corrupted the Church. It would never recover. Following Constantine, the Church was locked into apostasy. There have been temporary revivals from time to time, yet, the main body of the Church has remained committed to apostasy as it is today.

---

[5]Mark 12:30

[6]Walker, *A History of the Christian Church*, pg. 101

Evolution of Church Doctrine

In order to demonstrate the evolvement of Christian thought, we will consider four specific doctrines. We will include numerous direct quotes from early Christian leaders who spoke of these subjects. In this way we can readily see how the Church position evolved.

Definition of God

The Bible is the written revelation of God to man. There are many names of God revealed in the Scriptures. Perhaps the most significant one was revealed to Moses at Mt. Sinai in the incident of the "Burning Bush". God declared that His name is,

אֶהְיֶה אֲשֶׁר אֶהְיֶה -- "I Will Be that which I Will Be".[7]

This name is extremely important because it declares that God is not only "self-existent" and "sovereign" but, in addition, He declared by this name that He is not definable. We can say that we understand something about God but we can never assert that we have defined God's being. Other names of God revealed in the Bible include *the Creator*, *El Shaddai*, and *the God of Abraham, the God of Isaac and the God of Jacob*.

God also revealed His intention of sending a very special anointed king who would ultimately reign over the whole world. This king eventually became seen as the Messiah. Of course we maintain that Jesus is that Messiah or uniquely anointed king. In the New Testament, Jesus is referred to as *the only begotten of the Father*, *the Word*, *the Way*, *the Truth*, *the Life*, *the Resurrection*, etc.

Throughout the New Testament we hear the terminology concerning God the Father and our Lord, Jesus, the Messiah. From time to time there is a reference made to the Holy Spirit.

---

[7]Exodus 3:14

We can witness the terminology used in the greetings of the New Testament letters:

> "Paul, a bond-servant of Christ Jesus, called as an apostle, set apart for the gospel of God, which He promised beforehand through His prophets in the holy Scriptures, concerning His son, who was born of a descendant of David according to the flesh, who was declared the Son of God with power by the resurrection from the dead, according to the Spirit of holiness, Jesus Christ our Lord, through whom we have received grace and apostleship to bring about the obedience of faith among all the Gentiles, for His name's sake, among whom you also are the called of Jesus Christ; to all who are beloved of God in Rome, called as saints: Grace to you and peace from God our Father and the Lord Jesus Christ".[8]
>
> "Paul, an apostle of Christ Jesus by the will of God, to the saints who are at Ephesus, and who are faithful in Christ Jesus. Grace to you and peace from God our Father and the Lord Jesus Christ".[9]
>
> "Paul, an apostle of Christ Jesus according to the commandment of God our Savior, and of Christ Jesus, who is our hope; to Timothy, my true child in the faith: Grace, mercy and peace from God the Father and Christ Jesus our Lord".[10]

---

[8]Romans 1:1-7
[9]Ephesians 1:1-2
[10]I Timothy 1:1-2

> "James, a bond-servant of God and of the Lord Jesus Christ, to the twelve tribes who are dispersed abroad, greetings".[11]
>
> "Peter, an apostle of Jesus Christ, to those who reside as aliens, scattered throughout Pontus, Galatia, Cappadocia, Asia, and Bithynia, who are chosen according to the foreknowledge of God the Father, by the sanctifying work of the Spirit, that you may obey Jesus Christ and be sprinkled with His blood: May grace and peace be yours in fullest measure".[12]
>
> "John to the seven churches that are in Asia: grace to you and peace, from Him who is and who was and who is to come; and from the seven Spirits who are before His throne; and from Jesus Christ, the faithful witness, the first-born of the dead, and the ruler of the kings of the earth. To Him who loves us, and released us from our sins by His blood, and He has made us to be a kingdom, priests to His God and Father; to Him be the glory and the dominion forever and ever. Amen".[13]

The book of Revelation gives us a number of specific pictures of the Holy One and His Messiah. Worship is pictured in Revelation 5:11-14. Worship is directed to "He who sits on the throne" and to the "Lamb". In the Ages to come (the New Creation) glory and honor will be brought to the city of New Jerusalem. The Holy One and the Lamb will dwell in the city. The Lamb is always described as being in subjection (under the authority of) to the Holy One. We as believers find our acceptance in God's presence in Messiah Jesus. Yet Biblical

---

[11]James 1:1
[12]I Peter 1:1-2
[13]Revelation 1:4-6

worship and service are ultimately directed to the Holy One of Israel, the One who declared that "He would be that which He would be".

Notice that in these greetings, reference is made to God the Father and to "our" Lord, Jesus Christ (the Messiah). There are isolated references to the "Spirit". The pattern set here in the New Testament should have been followed by the Church in all subsequent generations. However, we will show that the Church of the second, third, fourth and fifth centuries departed from this pattern and developed, by means of Gentile philosophies, a detailed definition of God referred to as the '*Holy Trinity*'. By doing so, the post Biblical Church violated the most significant, revealed name of God, "I will be that which I will be",[14] which is understood to imply that man cannot define God and is forbidden to attempt to do so.

The language of the second century Church leaders follows closely that of the New Testament. Polycarp's epistle to the Philippians (~110 AD) sounds much like Paul:

> "Polycarp, and the presbyters that are with him, to the church of God sojourning at Philippi: Mercy unto you and peace from God Almighty, and from the Lord Jesus Christ, our Savior, be multiplied".[15]

Clement, bishop of Rome, (~110 AD) uses similar terminology:

> "The Church of God which sojourns at Rome, to the Church of God sojourning at Corinth, to them that are called and sanctified by the word of God, through our Lord Jesus Christ: Grace unto you, and peace, from Almighty God through Jesus Christ, be multiplied".[16]

Ignatius, the bishop of the Church at Antioch wrote (~110 AD):

---

[14]Exodus 3:14
[15]Epistle of Polycarp to the Philippians, 1:1-2
[16]The First Epistle of Clement to the Corithians, 1:1

> "Ignatius, who is also called Theophorus, to the Church which is at Ephesus, in Asia, deservedly most happy, being blessed in the greatness and fulness of God the Father, and predestinated before the beginning of time, that it should be always for an enduring and unchangeable glory, being united and elected through the true passion by the will of the Father, and Jesus Christ, our God: Abundant happiness through Jesus Christ, and His undefiled grace".[17]

Note that Ignatius departs somewhat from general New Testament usage when he uses the expression "Jesus Christ, our God".

Justin (~150 AD) used terminology in which we can discern the developing pattern that will be followed in subsequent centuries:

> "Hence are we called atheists. And we confess that we are atheists, so far as gods of this sort are concerned, but not with respect to the most true God, the Father of righteousness and temperance and the other virtues, who is free from all impurity. But both Him, and the Son (who came forth from Him and taught us these things, and the host of the other good angels who follow and are made like to Him), and the prophetic Spirit, we worship and adore, knowing them in reason and truth, and declaring without grudging to every one who wishes to learn, as we have been taught".[18]

Justin continues this pattern as he declared:

> "For, in the name of God, the Father and Lord of the universe, and of our Saviour Jesus Christ, and of the Holy Spirit, they then receive the

---

[17]The Epistle of Ignatius to the Ephisians, 1:1-3

[18]The First Apology of Justin, chapter VI

> washing with water".[19]

Irenaeus, Bishop of Lyons, (~ 180 AD) maintains a more Biblical pattern than his contemporaries. He wrote:

> "The Father is indeed above all, and He is the Head of Christ; but the Word is through all things, and is Himself the Head of the Church; while the Spirit is in us all, and He is the living water, which the Lord grants to those who rightly believe in Him, and love Him, and who know that there is one Father, who is above all, and through all, and in us all".[20]

Origen in the third century expressed similar terminology concerning God the Father and Jesus the Messiah and, in addition, he expressed uncertainty concerning the Holy Spirit:

> "Then, thirdly the apostles related that the Holy Spirit was associated in honour and dignity with the Father and the Son. But in His case it is not clearly distinguished whether He is to be regarded as born or innate, or also as a Son of God or not; for these are points which have to be inquired into out of sacred Scripture according to the best of our ability, and which demand careful investigation".[21]

Later he uses terminology that would become foundational to the philosophy of the Holy Trinity:

> "From all which we learn that the person of the Holy Spirit was of such authority and dignity, that saving baptism was not complete except by the authority of the most excellent Trinity of them all, i.e., by the naming of Father, Son, and Holy Spirit, and by joining to the unbeggotten God the Father, and to His only-begotten Son, the name

---

[19]ibid., chapter LXI

[20]Iranaeus Against Heresies, chapter XVIII

[21]Origin, *De Prinapiis*, preface.

> also of the Holy Spirit".[22]

In the writings of Tertullian in *The Apology* (~200 AD) we hear the terminology that would be adopted at the Council of Nicea:

> "We have been taught that He proceeds forth from God, and in that procession He is generated; so that He is the Son of God, and is called God from unity of substance with God. For God, too, is a Spirit. Even when the ray is shot from the sun, it is still part of the parent mass; the sun will still be in the ray, because it is a ray of the sun--there is no division of substance, but merely an extension. Thus Christ is Spirit of Spirit, and God of God, as light of light is kindled".[23]

Tertullian argues against the concept that the "three manifestations of God" are "one person":

> "in the case of the heresy, which supposes itself to possess the pure truth, in thinking that one cannot believe in One Only God in any other way than by saying that the Father, the Son, and the Holy Ghost are the very selfsame Person. As if in this way also one were not All, in that All are of One, by unity (that is) of substance; while the mystery of the dispensation is still guarded, which distributes the Unity into a Trinity, placing in their order the Three Persons -- the Father, the Son, and the Holy Ghost; three, however, not in condition, but in degree; not in substance, but in form; not in power, but in aspect; yet of one substance, and of one condition, and of one power, inasmuch as He is one God, from whom these degrees and forms and aspects are reckoned, under the name of the Father, and of

---

[22]ibid, Book I, chapter III
[23]Tertullian, *The Apology*, chapter XXI

the Son, and of the Holy Ghost".[24]

It should be obvious to the reader that Tertullian had long since departed from any fidelity to the language of the New Testament and was advancing his argument based on some philosophical thought process unrelated to Biblical revelation.

Arius in the fourth century preached that the Son was a created being. According to the account of Eusebius, Arius maintained,

> "that God has not always been a Father, and that there was a time when the Son was not; that the Son is a creature like the others; the he is mutable by his nature; that by his free will he chose to remain virtuous, but that he might change like others. He said that Jesus Christ was not true God, but divine by participation, like all others to whom the name of God is attributed. He added, that he was not the substantial Word of the Father, and his proper wisdom, by which he had made all things, but that he was himself made by the eternal wisdom; that he is foreign in every thing from the substance of the Father; that we were not made for him, but he for us, when it was the pleasure of God, who was before alone, to create us; that he was made by the will of God, as others are, having no previous existence at all, since he is not a proper and natural production of the Father, but as effect of his grace. The Father, he continued, is invisible to the Son, and the Son cannot know him perfectly; nor, indeed, can he know his own substance".[25]

The dispute arising from the view expressed by Arius

---

[24]Tertullian, *Against Praxeas*, chapter II

[25]Isaac Boyle, *The Council of Nice*, Baker Book House, Grand Rapids, Michigan, pg. 13

caused Emperor Constantine to assemble the First General Council of the Church at Nicea in Asia Minor. In response to the views expressed by Arius, the Council concluded that the "Son is consubstantial with the Father", making use of the Greek word ὁμοούσιον. This was understood:

> "to signify that the Son is not only like the Father, but so similar that he may be called with propriety the same; and implies that the resemblance and immutability of the Son is different from that which is affirmed of us, and which we acquire by the practice of virtue, and the observation of the divine commands".[26]

This led to the adoption of the church creed associated with the Council of Nicea:

> "We believe in one God, Almighty Father, maker of all things seen and unseen, and in one Lord Jesus Christ, the Son of God, begotten of the Father and only begotten that is, from the essence of the Father, God from God, Light from Light, True God from True God, begotten, not made, of one essence with the Father. Through whom all things were made, both the things in heaven and the things upon the earth, Who for us men and for our salvation, descended and became flesh and became man, suffered and arose on the third day, and ascended into the heavens, and is coming to judge living and dead. We believe also in the Holy Spirit".[27]

This creed left the position of the Holy Spirit in question. Subsequent synods concluded that the Holy Spirit was consubstantial with the Father and with the Son. This position was adopted in the Second General Council of 381 AD. Therefore the foundation for the definition of the Holy Trinity

---

[26]ibid., pg. 20

[27]Robert Baker, *A Summary of Christian History*, Broadman, Nashville, TN, pg. 62

of Christianity was laid.

Probably one of the most influential Church fathers was Augustine of Hippo. Augustine was responsible for making the concept of the Holy Trinity popular particularly in the Western Church. His view of the "Holy Trinity" is stated in his work entitled, *On The Trinity*. He summarized the view of the Trinity as:

> "this doctrine, that the Father, and the Son, and the Holy Spirit intimate a divine unity of one and the same substance in an indivisible equality; and therefore that they are not three Gods, but one God: although the Father hath begotten the Son, and so He who is the Father is not the Son; and the Son is begotten by the Father, and so He who is the Son is not the Father; and the Holy Spirit is neither the Father nor the Son, but only the Spirit of the Father and of the Son, Himself also co-equal with the Father and the Son, and pertaining to the unity of the Trinity".[28]

This is, of course, very difficult to understand. Obviously this doctrinal-type statement is aimed at answering the pressing theological debate of the fourth and fifth centuries and has little to do with Biblical revelation. This statement of the "Holy Trinity" has been accepted since the time of Augustine. It remains the test of orthodoxy to this day.

Note that the full definition of the Christian Holy Trinity occurred gradually over a period of about 300 years. This resulted from a gradual departure from the specific nomenclature of the New Testament aided by philosophical speculation. To some degree this "defining" of the Christian God was a reaction to unbiblical teaching. This was true of the Gnostics and of Arius. What is most important for us to see is that church leaders of the second, third, fourth and fifth centuries ignored the most basic name of God revealed to Moses, "I will

---

[28]Augustine, *On The Trinity*, Book I, chapter IV

be that which I will be". Instead of maintaining a reverence for the Name of God which is characteristic of Jewish thought, church leaders freely speculated about every conceivable aspect of the Name of God. As church leaders defined more and more precisely their concept of God; they violated this most basic and fundamental aspect of God's name and the fundamental principle that God declared from the beginning -- that He cannot be defined. There would be nothing wrong with stating that in the New Testament era, God has been experienced as Father, as Son and as Holy Spirit. We believe that

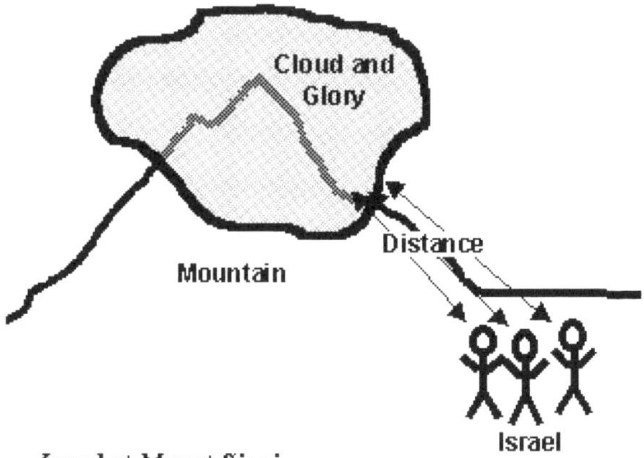

Israel at Mount Sinai

the New Testament Scriptures would support such a position. But to declare the specific make-up of God and the detailed interrelations of God is simply unscriptural.

The doctrine of the Holy Trinity has become the most defining doctrine of Christianity. Indeed, it is the ultimate test of orthodoxy. Nevertheless, it must be rejected on the basis that it is unscriptural even though it has been generally accepted for 1,500 years. It must be replaced with the nomenclature revealed in the writings of the New Testament in order for believers to return to the Hebraic roots and function of that early church.

The evolution of the doctrine of the Holy Trinity can be

understood by considering how men have reacted to the revealing of God throughout Biblical history. When Israel was led to Mt. Sinai following their exodus from Egypt, God descended upon the mountain and was manifested by a cloud, thunder, lighting, earthquakes, and the sound of a great trumpet. Israel (each individual) heard the voice of God speaking the ten commandments to him. Most would envision a booming voice coming from the cloud as portrayed in popular Hollywood versions of the story. Later, Elijah came to the same place[29] and recognized God speaking to him in a "silent, small voice". I believe that God spoke in just this way to every Israeli at Mt. Sinai. The Israelis were terrified of the obvious intimacy with God. They understood the implications of their individual unholiness contrasted with the holiness of God. As a result, they petitioned Moses to hear from and to speak to God on their behalf. They would communicate through Moses. Moses actually ascended the mountain and entered the cloud. Moses in this way acted as a "Messiah" functioning between God and His people. At any rate, the people saw God and experienced Him from a distance; they were more comfortable with this arrangement. Israel's relationship with God remains so today, God is in their midst, keeping and guiding them, but on a personal level, He is at a distance from them, on the mountain.

Now we come to the New Testament era. On the Day of Pentecost (*Yom Hashavuot*) the Holy Spirit descended on the disciples in the upper room. They were filled with the Holy Spirit. From the description of the events of Mt. Sinai some 1,400 years earlier, the disciples entered the cloud as Moses had before them. They experienced God in an intimate way as they were filled with the Holy Spirit. Later, after Paul had experienced the same thing, he described the phenomena that I will call "*introspection of God*". Paul wrote:

"For to us God revealed them through the Spirit;

---

[29] I Kings 19:11-13

Early Church on Pentecost / Yom Hashavuot

> for the Spirit searches all things, even the depths of God. For who among men knows the thoughts of a man except the spirit of the man, which is in him? Even so the thoughts of God no one knows except the Spirit of God. Now we have received, not the spirit of the world, but the Spirit who is from God, that we might know the things freely given to us by God".[30]

The writers of the New Testament wrote from the perspective of the cloud. They had been born again (brought into a new spiritual perception by the Holy Spirit) so they readily identified with the term so commonly used by Jesus for God -- Father. They experienced the being of Jesus whom they perceived as the Messiah who they saw resurrected and glorified. They understood according to the accounts given concerning his conception that he had been begotten by God (hence the terminology of John, the only begotten of the Father). They referred to him as the Son. They each experienced the infilling of the Holy Spirit, so they, of course, spoke of the Spirit. Yet, from the New Testament, it is readily discernable that the expression "God" or "Heavenly Father" was understood to

---

[30] I Corithians 2:10-12

mean that unique Being revealed throughout the Bible as the Holy One of Israel, the God of creation, the God of Abraham, the God of Isaac and the God of Jacob, the One who declared, "I will be that which I will be". The writers of the New Testament spoke in a very limited way of the relationship of the Father and the Son, but not in the degree of detail that could be considered comprehensive. Details of that relationship remained a mystery open only to the believer who was filled with the Holy Spirit and, therefore, given the capacity of "introspection of God"[31].

Many of the church leaders of the second through fifth

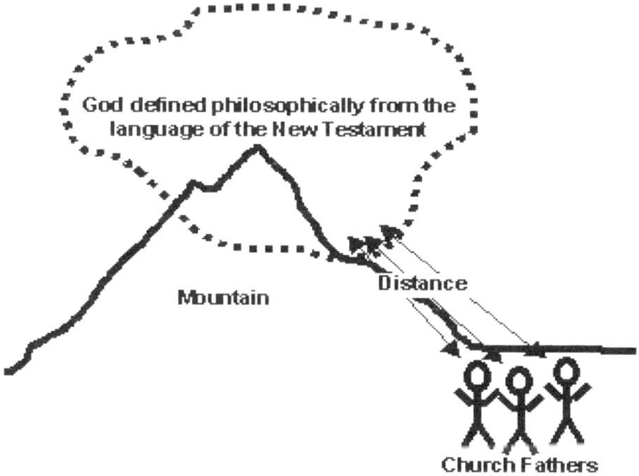

Constantinian Church

centuries were obviously more strongly influenced by Gentile philosophies than by Biblical revelation. Judging from their writings, little evidence is demonstrated that they were "born again". If they were, their minds were so captivated by philosophy that they would have little if any capacity for "introspection of God". It appears as if they and the Church following them resorted to worship of a god that could be seen

---

[31] I Corithians 2:10-12

at a distance (there is little evidence of the intimate life common in the first century church). The church leaders defined this god using the intimate terminology of the New Testament and subsequently defined his being. This god was seen as "universal". The work of god was defined as saving a people from all the earth. So the Church of this early post-Biblical era embraced the new religion of Christianity, worshiping a god defined for them by Church theologians, one who was a "universal" god defined with the terminology used by the writers of the New Testament. This new god was worshiped at a distance.

Replacement Theology

Unlike the evolution of the definition of God which took almost three centuries, the development of a theological position for the replacement of Israel with the Church occurred very quickly. Again this is in complete disregard of the simple, straight-forward teachings of the Scriptures. The covenant that God made with Abraham was eternal:

> "And I will establish My covenant between Me and you and your descendants after you throughout their generations for an everlasting covenant, to be God to you and to your descendants after you. And I will give to you and to your descendants after you, the land of your sojournings, all the land of Canaan, for an everlasting possession; and I will be their God".[32]

The covenant that God cut with Abraham was restated and enhanced at Mt. Sinai. Here, God cut His covenant with the nation of Israel which He had recently delivered from Egypt. Israel inherited the land of promise in the days of Joshua ben Nun, but the history of the first Kingdom era (1400 BC - 586 BC) was turbulent, filled with sin and judgment. The ultimate judgment of God on His people was to expel them from the

---

[32]Genesis 17:7-8

land. Contrary to the assumption of the early Church fathers, rejection or divorce of His people was never an option considered by God.

Probably the most difficult period in the history of Israel was the time at the end of the first Temple era as God prepared to eject His people from the land. Jeremiah was called to be the prophet of record that would give witness to what God was doing, to stir hope in Israel for the future and to give to Israel a "word of faith" for the future. On the basis of what the people observed as the Babylonians prevailed in Jerusalem and Judea, they concluded that God had divorced them. Yet, Jeremiah declared:

> "Have you not observed what this people have spoken, saying, 'The two families which the Lord chose, He has rejected them'? Thus they despise My people, no longer are they as a nation in their sight. Thus says the Lord, 'If My covenant for day and night stand not, and the fixed patterns of heaven and earth I have not established, then I would reject the descendants of Jacob and David My servant, not taking from his descendants rulers over the descendants of Abraham, Isaac, and Jacob. But I will restore their fortunes and will have mercy on them'".[33]

Two observations are crucial concerning this statement of Jeremiah. First, God stated in a most clear and definite way that He would never reject (cut-off, divorce) his people Israel, the descendants of Abraham, Isaac and Jacob. A second important point concerns God's statement relative to David. David represents the house of anointing within Israel, the anointed branch. Jesus became the fulfillment of this branch as the uniquely anointed one. The Church was later joined to Jesus as a part of this phenomena. God declared that this branch would never be cut off either. Note that these two

---

[33]Jeremiah 33:24-26

houses are Israel and the Church. This precludes one replacing the other.

In the New Testament, Paul uses the strongest possible language to confirm what had been stated earlier by Jeremiah. Paul says:

> "I say then, God has not rejected His people, has He? May it never be".[34]

and,

> "I say then, they did not stumble so as to fall, did they? May it never be!"[35]

and,

> "From the standpoint of the gospel they are enemies for your sake, but from the standpoint of God's choice they are beloved for the sake of the fathers; for the gifts and the calling of God are irrevocable".[36]

Therefore, the Biblical position on the eternal nature of God's covenant with His people is extremely clear. Actually nothing has been left to interpretation concerning this matter. Israel's active, elect position is strongly maintained both in the Hebrew and Messianic Scriptures.

Shortly after the life and ministry of Messiah Jesus, Jerusalem and Judea were again overrun by a foreign army, the Romans, and the second Temple era came to a close. There was a continuing struggle between Israel and Rome from 66 AD until the suppression of the Bar Kochba Revolt in 135 AD. The Romans completely prevailed over Israel; the remnant of Jews in the land of Israel either fled or were killed or sold into slavery. Many fled the land to join their brothers in the dispersion while only a tiny remnant managed to remain in the land.

From the standpoint of an outside observer, it would appear that Israel was finished; the national humiliation was

---

[34]Romans 11:1a
[35]Romans 11:11a
[36]Romans 11:28-29

complete. It is from this position, in total disregard to stated Biblical fact, that church leaders drew their conclusions concerning Israel. Ignatius, Bishop of Antioch, wrote (~110 AD):

> "It is absurd to speak of Jesus Christ with the tongue, and to cherish in the mind a Judaism which has now come to an end. For where there is Christianity there cannot be Judaism. For Christ is one, in whom every nation that believes, and every tongue that confesses, is gathered unto God. And those that were of a stony heart have become the children of Abraham, the friend of God; and in his seed all those have been blessed who were ordained to eternal life in Christ".[37]

Tertullian (~200 AD) stated that:

> "In former times the Jews enjoyed much of God's favour, when the fathers of their race were noted for their righteousness and faith . . . But how deeply they have sinned, puffed up to their fall with a false trust in their noble ancestors, turning from God's way into a way of sheer impiety, though they themselves should refuse to admit it, their present national ruin would afford sufficient proof. Scattered abroad, a race of wanderers, exiles from their own land and clime, they roam over the whole world without either a human or a heavenly king, not possessing even the stranger's right to set so much as a simple footstep in their native country. The sacred writers withal, in giving previous warning of these things, all with equal clearness ever declared that, in the last days of the world, God would, out of every nation, and people, and country, choose

[37]Epistle of Ignatius to the Magnesians, chapter X

> for Himself more faithful worshippers, upon whom He would bestow His grace, and that indeed in ampler measure, in keeping with the enlarged capacities of a nobler dispensation".[38]

Origin (~200 AD) drew the same conclusion as Tertullian based on the apparent judgment of Israel carried out by the Romans. He declared:

> "One fact, then which proves that Jesus was something divine and sacred, is this, that Jews should have suffered on His account now for a lengthened time calamities of such severity. And we say with confidence that they will never be restored to their former condition. For they committed a crime of the most unhallowed kind, in conspiring against the Saviour of the human race in that city where they offered up to God a worship containing the symbols of mighty mysteries. It accordingly behooved that city where Jesus underwent these sufferings to perish utterly, and the Jewish nation to be overthrown, and the invitation to happiness offered them by God to pass to others, -- the Christians".[39]

Cyprian, Bishop of Carthage, (~250 AD) repeated the same position:

> "First of all, favour with God was given to the Jews. Thus they of old were righteous . . . But subsequently becoming neglectful of discipline, proud, and puffed up with confidence in their fathers, they despised the divine precepts, and lost the favour conferred upon them" and, "God would gather to Himself from every nation, and people, and place, worshippers much better in obedience and stronger in faith, who would draw from the divine gift that mercy which the Jews

---

[38]Tertullian, *The Apology*, chapter XXI

[39]Origen, *Against Celsus*, Book IV, chapter XXII

> had received and lost by despising their religious ordinances".[40]

Note that no Scriptural evidence was set forth in confidently declaring that Israel had been cut off and replaced by the Church. Evidently the humiliation suffered by Israel was so complete that church leaders never seriously considered that there might be a different explanation for the observed situation. They simply concluded that Israel *was* cut off and that God had redirected His favor to the Church. Hence the Church was seen as replacing Israel. It was the "New Israel". By the fourth Century, Constantine openly ridiculed the Jewish people and exhorted the Church to separate themselves completely from them. Constantine convened the First General Council of the Church at Nicea in 325 AD. He controlled the agenda of the Council to insure that the Council's conclusion benefitted his goal. Following the Council, Constantine wrote concerning its proceedings. Concerning the Jews, he said:

> "And truly, in the first place, it seemed to every one a most unworthy thing that we should follow the custom of the Jews in the celebration of this most holy solemnity, who, polluted wretches! having stained their hands with a nefarious crime, are justly blinded in their minds. It is fit, therefore, that rejecting the practice of this people, we should perpetuate to all future ages the celebration of this rite, in a more legitimate order, which we have kept from the first day of our Lord's passion even to the present times. Let us then have nothing in common with the most hostile rabble of the Jews. We have received another method from the Saviour. A more lawful and proper course is open to our most holy religion. In pursuing this course with a unani-

[40]Cyprian, *The Treatises of Cyprian*, Treatise VI, chapters X-XI

> mous consent, let us withdraw ourselves, my much honored brethren, from that most odious fellowship".[41]

The Law

One of the foundational characteristics of the Hebrew Scripture revelation is the *Torah* or Law. Revealed through Moses at Mt. Sinai, the Law became the constitution for Israel. The Law prescribed those things necessary to maintain proper relationship with God and with man. The Law is the only code which has the stamp of divine approval. Incorporated within the Law is the system for sacrifices. Sacrifices provide a means to overcome sin and, hence, are the mechanism for God's grace to be shown to His people. Some aspects of the Law deal specifically with God's people in God's Land; however, most of the Law is easily understood and generally applicable.

Israel has correctly given great emphasis to the Law. The Law is the teacher; it teaches the way of right living. The Law confronts wrong attitudes and behaviors in men. The Law prescribes the manner of life that a righteous person should live.

Throughout the centuries, there developed within Israel a variety of interpretations of how to apply the Law to daily life. At the end of the Second Temple Era, the *Oral Tradition* (The Oral Tradition in written form, the *Mishna*, along with its commentary, the *Gemora*, became the *Talmud*) had been developed which gave detailed interpretation of how to apply the Law. Various schools of thought developed arguing how best to interpret and apply the Oral Tradition. Throughout the centuries there have been movements like the Karaites which advocated a return to the simple interpretation of the Law without the Oral Tradition. Jesus introduced and taught still another approach to the Law. He said,

---

[41]Boyle, *The Council Of Nice-Another Letter of Constantine*, page 52

> "Do not think that I came to abolish the Law or the Prophets; I did not come to abolish, but to fulfill. For truly I say to you, until heaven and earth pass away, not the smallest letter or stroke shall pass away from the Law, until all is accomplished. Whoever then annuls one of the least of these commandments, and so teaches others, shall be called least in the kingdom of heaven; but whoever keeps and teaches them, he shall be called great in the kingdom of heaven".[42]

Jesus' approach to the Law was to be filled with the Holy Spirit and, therefore, see as God sees, feel as God feels, assume the same priorities as God Himself does. This Jesus called fulfilling the Law. Later Paul advocated an identical approach. He exhorted the Roman church:

> "in order that the requirement of the Law might be fulfilled in us, who do not walk according to the flesh, but according to the Spirit".[43]

Paul continued to demonstrate that he was observant of the Law throughout his life .[44] In spite of these stated positions of Paul concerning his attitude on the Law, much misunderstanding has arisen over Paul's statement "we are not under the Law". Paul meant that it is impossible to justify ourselves by observing commandments, i.e., God has provided a means for our justification through the atoning death of Messiah Jesus. This is an accomplished fact to which we cannot add or take away anything. Paul also meant by this statement that he had discovered that he could not measure up to the requirements of the Law by sheer determined observance. Only by being filled with the Holy Spirit and living in close communion with God in Messiah Jesus could he truly fulfill the Law. This then was the attitude of Jesus and the New

---

[42]Matthew 5:17-19
[43]Romans 8:4
[44]Acts 21:17-26

Testament church concerning the Law.

The Church of the second century quickly departed from this position regarding the Law. Ignatius, Bishop of Antioch, (~110 AD) wrote:

> "For if we still live according to the Jewish law, we acknowledge that we have not received grace".[45]

and,

> "Let us therefore no longer keep the Sabbath after the Jewish manner, and rejoice in days of idleness . . . And, after the observance of the Sabbath, let every friend of Christ keep the Lord's Day as a festival, the resurrection-day, the queen and chief of all the days (of the week)".[46]

Justin (~150 AD) wrote concerning Shabbat:

> "But Sunday is the day on which we all hold our common assembly, because it is the first day on which God, having wrought a change in the darkness and matter, made the world; and Jesus Christ our Saviour on the same day rose from the dead".[47]

and, in his dialogue with a Jewish philosopher, he argued:

> "But we do not trust through Moses or through the law; for then we would do the same as yourselves. But now -- (for I have read that there shall be a final law, and a covenant, the chiefest of all, which it is now incumbent on all men to observe, as many as are seeking after the inheritance of God. For the law promulgated on Horeb is now old, and belongs to yourselves alone; but this is for all universally. Now, law placed against law has abrogated that which is

---

[45]Ignatius, Epistle of the Magnesians, chapter VIII

[46]ibid., chapter IX

[47]Justin, *The First Apology*, chapter LXVII

> before it, and a covenant which comes after in like manner has put an end to the previous one; and an eternal and final law -- namely, Christ -- has been given to us, and the covenant is trustworthy, after which there shall be no law, no commandment, no ordinance...)".[48]

and,

> "For we too would observe the fleshly circumcision, and the Sabbaths, and in short all the feasts, if we did not know for what reason they were enjoined you, -- namely, on account of your transgressions and the hardness of your hearts".[49]

Irenaeus, Bishop of Lyons, wrote (~180 AD) concerning the Law:

> "The laws of bondage, however, were one by one promulgated to the people by Moses, suited for their instruction or for their punishment, as Moses himself declared: 'And the Lord commanded me at that time to teach you statutes and judgments'. These things, therefore, which were given for bondage, and for a sign to them, He cancelled by the new covenant of liberty".[50]

Please note the attitude reflected by Irenaeus compared to the view expressed by Jesus (quoted earlier), "Do not think that I came to abolish the Law".

Tertullian (~200 AD) imagined that a "new" law had been published by which Christians were to live:

> "In short, before the Law of Moses, written in stone-tables, I contend that there was a law unwritten, which was habitually understood naturally, and by the fathers was habitually kept."

---

[48]Justin, *Dialogue with Trypho*, chapter XI

[49]ibid, chapter XVIII

[50]Irenaeus, *Against Heresies*, Book IV, chapter XVI, paragraph 5.

and,

> "so that we are not to give heed to Moses' Law as to the primitive law, but as to a subsequent, which at a definite period God has set forth to the Gentiles too and, after repeatedly promising so to do through the prophets, has reformed for the better; and has premonished that it should come to pass that, just as 'the law was given through Moses' at a definite time, so it should be believed to have been temporarily observed and kept".[51]

and,

> "Who else, therefore, are understood but we, who, fully taught by the new law, observe these practices, -- the old law being obliterated, the coming of whose abolition the action itself demonstrates?"[52]

God's festivals (Shabbat, Passover, Shavuot, Yom Kippur and Sukkot - Leviticus 23:37) are a central feature of the Law. The Church devised new festivals to replace the "appointed times of the Lord". We have already seen that the Shabbat was changed from the last day of the week to the first day of the week. The celebration of the resurrection was changed from "First Fruits" to Easter. A controversy arose as early as 190 AD concerning the time when this festival was to be celebrated. The issue was dealt with at the first General Council of the Church at Nicea (325 AD). Eusebius gives his account of the proceedings:

> "The question relating to the observance of Easter, which was agitated in the time of Anicetus and Polycarp, and afterwards in that of Victor, was still undecided . . . It appears that the churches of Syria and Mesopotamia continued to follow the custom of the Jews, and celebrated Easter on the fourteenth day of the moon

[51]Tertullian, *An Answer to the Jews*, chapter II
[52]ibid., chapter III

> whether falling on Sunday or not. All the other churches observed that solemnity on Sunday only . . . Easter day was fixed on the Sunday immediately following the new moon which was nearest after the vernal equinox, because it is certain that our Saviour rose from the dead on the Sunday which next succeeded the passover of the Jews".[53]

Concerning the festival of Christmas, Walker writes:

> "January 6 came to be widely observed by the orthodox in the East as the birth and baptism of Jesus, 'Epiphany' referring to God's 'manifesting' Himself in these events . . . About the same time, the early fourth century, there developed in the West a distinctive nativity festival on December 25. The date was partly determined by the idea that the birth of the world occurred on the vernal equinox (March 25) and correspondingly its new birth in the Saviour would have been at the same moment. This was understood as the conception by the Virgin, and hence the actual birth would be nine months later, December 25. But perhaps even more the date was influenced by the fact that December 25 was a great pagan festival, that of Sol Invictus, which celebrated the victory of light over darkness and the lengthening of the sun's rays at the winter solstice".[54]

Therefore we conclude that the Church of the second -- fourth centuries embraced a "new law of liberty" which they envisioned had replaced the "old law of bondage", the Torah. This "new law" has *no* Scriptural basis whatsoever. Indeed, such a law is not even hinted at in the writings of the first century Church. Based on the words of Jesus and Paul,

---

[53]Boyle, *Council of Nice*, pg. 22-23

[54]Walker, *A History of the Christian Church*, pgs. 154-155

quoted previously, their concern was very much for the Torah. More striking is the fact that this "new law" is undefined. Therefore, the Church has evolved into a non-law position, again completely contrary to Scriptural revelation. Finally, the "appointed times of the Lord" were changed to new festivals to suit the purposes of the Church. This, also, was done completely contrary to Scriptural revelation.

Judgment and Exclusive Church Authority

From the beginning of the Scriptural record, man is seen as having fallen from his original position of blessing in the Garden of Eden. God said to man,

> "But from the tree of the knowledge of good and evil you shall not eat, for in the day that you eat from it you shall surely die".[55]

In the following chapter of the Bible, we see this death occurring; man was driven out of the garden, out from the presence of God. Death meant, evidently, separation from God's presence. Adam was separated from the sustaining life which flows from the presence of God. From this, and Biblical revelation in general, we conclude that death always means separation. It never means cessation of being as is accepted in contemporary thought. Physical death means separation from this physical universe. Paul wrote,

> "we are of good courage, I say, and prefer rather to be absent from the body and to be at home with the Lord".[56]

John, furthermore, spoke of the "second death". He meant by this expression: the final separation that can occur to a person who, after physical death, is separated eternally from God's New Creation following final judgment.

Very little is revealed in the Hebrew Scriptures concerning the concept of final judgment. Ezekiel spoke briefly of

[55]Genesis 2:17
[56]II Corithians 5:8

personal accountability.[57] Malachi spoke of a "Book of Remembrance" by which God would "distinguish between the righteous and the wicked, between one who serves God and one who does not serve Him".[58] It was not until the ministry of Messiah Jesus that the subject was brought into full focus. Jesus taught openly concerning the coming individual judgment and the universal applicability of it. He said:

> "Do not marvel at this; for an hour is coming, in which all who are in the tombs shall hear His voice, and shall come forth; those who did the good deeds to a resurrection of life, those who committed the evil deeds to a resurrection of judgment".[59]

Note that this statement is *universally* (all who are in the tombs) applicable. Note also that the basis for judgment is the *deeds of this life*. From this statement the assumption would have to be made that every person, Jewish as well as Gentile, would eventually stand before the God of Israel and be judged. In addition, we must assume that some Jews, as well as Gentiles, would be accepted into life and some Jews, as well as Gentiles, would be rejected unto death.

Paul treated the same subject of judgment. He stated that there was coming a day of wrath and revelation of the righteous judgment of God:

> "who will render to every man according to his deeds: to those who by perseverance in doing good seek for glory and honor and immortality, eternal life; but to those who are selfishly ambitious and do not obey the truth, but obey unrighteousness, wrath and indignation. There will be tribulation and distress for every soul of man who does evil, of the Jew first and also of the

---

[57]Ezekiel 18 and 33
[58]Malachi 3:16-18
[59]John 5:28-29

> Greek, but glory and honor and peace to every man who does good, to the Jew first and also to the Greek. For there is no partiality with God. For all who have sinned without the Law will also perish without the Law; and all who have sinned under the Law will be judged by the Law; for not the hearers of the Law are just before God, but the doers of the Law will be justified. For when Gentiles who do not have the Law do instinctively the things of the Law, these, not having the Law, are a law to themselves, in that they show the work of the Law written in their hearts, their conscience bearing witness, and their thoughts alternately accusing or else defending them on the day when, according to my gospel, God will judge the secrets of men through Christ Jesus".[60]

Again Paul's statement is universally applicable -- God will render to every man. The basis for judgment is those things done in this life. For those who are accepted by God (from either Jewish or Gentile backgrounds), God will grant eternal life. For those who are rejected by God (from either Jewish or Gentile backgrounds), God will grant wrath and indignation. Paul boldly declares that those who have not received specific revelation of God will be judged not on the standard of Torah but on the basis of natural revelation. Obviously, according to Paul's gospel, at least some of such people will be accepted by God into eternal life.

John saw a vision of a "great white throne" before which men would be judged. He said,

> "And I saw the dead, the great and the small, standing before the throne, and books were opened; and another book was opened, which is the book of life; and the dead were judged from the things which were written in the books,

---

[60]Romans 2:6-16

> according to their deeds. And the sea gave up the dead which were in it, and death and Hades gave up the dead which were in them; and they were judged, every one of them according to their deeds. And death and Hades were thrown into the lake of fire. This is the second death, the lake of fire. And if anyone's name was not found written in the book of life, he was thrown into the lake of fire".[61]

John's vision clearly includes all mankind from throughout the ages. The basis for judgment is the deeds done in this present life. Some are granted acceptance, i.e., eternal life; some are eternally rejected, i.e., the lake of fire.

This is the stated vision of ultimate accountability of all men to God. The early Church went forth preaching this message of accountability and proclaiming that:

> "God was in Christ reconciling the world to Himself not counting their trespasses against them".[62]

What was required of the person hearing this message? He simple turned from his former pagan lifestyle and walked upright before God. His former trespasses were forgiven; therefore, he could begin anew.

The early Church saw itself as an elect community sanctified by the Holy Spirit, specifically called to worship God, to train disciples (those brought into the elect community) and to proclaim the message of reconciliation to the world. To believers they proclaimed the message of the Kingdom of God; to the nations they proclaimed reconciliation to the God of the Scriptures.

We conclude from the Genesis account that Adam experienced death; he was driven out from the presence of God and was prohibited from approaching God on his own

---

[61]Revelation 20:12-15

[62]II Corithians 5:19

terms. All subsequent generations were born into this same condition, i.e., not one was born having an inherent relationship or communion with God. That had ended in the fall. Note that even though man could not approach God, God has approached man throughout the generations. This is the account given in the Bible.

God could have judged man immediately and found him guilty and sentenced him to the lake of fire. Actually, this would have seemed logical and just; however, God choose another way. First, He determined that all would not be condemned for the sin of Adam.
God proclaimed through the prophet Ezekiel:

> "'What do you mean by using this proverb concerning the land of Israel saying, "The fathers eat the sour grapes, but the children's teeth are set on edge"? As I live', declares the Lord God, 'you are surely not going to use this proverb in Israel anymore. Behold, all souls are Mine; the soul of the father as well as the soul of the son is Mine. The soul who sins will die'".[63]

Every person would live out his life, in adversity (which he inherited due to the sin of Adam), and would demonstrate by his consistent lifestyle whether he loved God or not. One would be rejected only if he individually demonstrated that he was selfishly ambitious and disobedient to the truth. Some might argue that this is divinely unjust, yet, this is the manner chosen by God. Ultimately, the price for this mercy was paid for through the atoning death of Messiah Jesus.[64]

This view of judgment changed slowly in the post-Biblical era. Gradually, the Church redefined its mission and its vision of itself. Eventually the Church became seen as an "ark" in which God was rescuing some souls. The mission of the Church became the salvation of souls. We will see in the writings of Cyprian the view of the Church as the ark. Later, in

---

[63]Ezekiel 18:2-4
[64]Romans 5:18

the writings of Augustine, the argument is set forth that every soul must come into the Church or else it is eternally doomed (doctrine of absolute depravity). This became the prevailing view of the Church and remains so today. As a result, the Church claimed absolute authority over every human soul; it had the power of life or death. Final judgment was precluded by the Church - if one was in the Church he was saved; if he were not in the Church he was doomed. This obviously is contrary to Biblical revelation.

As with other subjects discussed in the section, we will trace the developing thought concerning judgment through the writings of the Church fathers. Ignatius took a radical view for his day (~110 AD). He declared:

> "Let no man deceive himself. Unless he believes that Christ Jesus has lived in the flesh, and shall confess His cross and passion, and the blood which He shed for the salvation of the world, he shall not obtain eternal life, whether he be a king, or a priest, or a ruler, or a private person, a master or a servant, a man or a woman".[65]

Justin (~150 AD) assumed a more Biblical position. He wrote:

> "...we hold this view, that it is alike impossible for the wicked, the covetous, the conspirator, and for the virtuous, to escape the notice of God, and that each man goes to everlasting punishment or salvation according to the value of his actions".[66]

and,

> "...we believe...that every man will suffer punishment in eternal fire according to the merit of his deed, and will render account according to the power he has received from God, as Christ intimated when He said, 'to whom God has given

---

[65]Ignatius, *Epistle to the Smyrnaeans*, chapter VI
[66]Justin, *The First Apology*, chapter XII

more, of him shall more be required'".[67]

Irenaeus (~180 AD) maintained a Biblical view, stating:

"...He should execute just judgment towards all; that He may send 'spiritual wickednesses', and the angels who transgressed and became apostates, together with the ungodly, and unrighteous, and wicked, and profane among men, into everlasting fire; but may, in the exercise of His grace, confer immortality on the righteous, and holy, and those who have kept His commandments, and have persevered in His love, some from the beginning [of their Christian course], and others from [the date of] their repentance, and may surround them with everlasting glory".[68]

Origin (~200 AD) continued this same theme:

"...Let them beware of doing ought which is displeasing to the Creator of this universe, of the soul and its intelligent principle; and let them rest assured that punishment shall be inflicted on the wicked, and rewards shall be bestowed upon the righteous, by Him who deals with every one as he deserves, and who will proportion His rewards to the good that each has done, and to the account of himself that he is able to give. And let all men know that the good shall be advanced to a higher state, and that the wicked shall be delivered over to sufferings and torments, in punishment of their licentiousness and depravity, their cowardice, timidity, and all their follies".[69]

Tertullian (~220 AD) stated:

"Again, we affirm that a judgment has been

---

[67]ibid., chapter XVII

[68]Irenaeus, *Against Heresies*, Book I, chapter X

[69]Origin, *Against Celsus*, Book VIII, chapter LII

> ordained by God according to the merits of every man" and "By the award of the judgment, we say that the wicked will have to spend an eternity in endless fire, the pious and innocent in a region of bliss".[70]

Cyprian (~250 AD) functioned at a time of great stress in the Church. The Church had suffered great persecution under the ruler Decius (249-251 AD). Many had fallen away and denied the faith to avoid persecution. After the persecution ended, many of these wanted to return to the Church. There was much controversy as to how this question should be handled. It is in this context that Cyprian defined the Church as an "ark" in which alone salvation could be found. He said:

> "Whoever he may be, and whatever he may be, he who is not in the Church of Christ is not a Christian".[71]

and,

> "there is no salvation out of the Church".[72]

Actually, Cyprian was not dealing directly with the judgment issue but his position and vision of the Church as an "ark" was embraced by the Church. The Church assumed great authority with these statements.

Finally, in the fifth century there was a doctrinal clash between Augustine, Bishop of Hippo and Pelagius. Pelagius argued that a human being was born in the same position as Adam, hence, he denied the consequences of the fall. Augustine argued the opposite position and, in response, developed a position that has been referred to as the *absolute depravity* of man. He argued that man was in such a position that without a unique saving experience he is doomed to the second death, i.e., eternal rejection and torment. Augustine argued that the first resurrection spoken of by John in the

---

[70]Tertullian, *AD Nationes*, Book I, chapter XIX
[71]Cyprian, *Epistle LI*, chapter XXIV
[72]Cyprian, Epistle LXXII, chapter XXI

book of Revelation,[73] actually pertains to being "born again" in this present life:

> "As, then, there are two regenerations, of which I have already made mention, -- the one according to faith, and which takes place in the present life by means of baptism; the other according to the flesh, and which shall be accomplished in its incorruption and immortality by means of the great and final judgment, -- so are there also two resurrections, -- the one the first and spiritual resurrection, which has place in this life, and preserves us from coming into the second death; the other the second, which does not occur now, but in the end of the world and which is of the body, not of the soul, and which by the last judgment shall dismiss some into the second death, others into that life which has no death".[74]

According to Augustine, the second resurrection spoken of by John, is a bodily resurrection and will result in immediate confinement into the Lake of Fire.

> "And therefore, when the day of the bodily resurrection arrives, they shall come out of their graves, not to life, but to judgment, namely to damnation, which is called the second death. For whosoever has not lived until the thousand years be finished, i.e., during this whole time in which the first resurrection is going on, -- whosoever has not heard the voice of the Son of God, and passed from death to life, -- that man shall certainly in the second resurrection, the resurrection of the flesh, pass with his flesh into the second death".[75]

Obviously, Augustine, with this interpretation, set forth the

---

[73]Revelation 20:4-6
[74]Augustine, *The City of God*, Book XX, chapter VI
[75]ibid., chapter IX

doctrine of “Post-Millennialism” since he spiritualized the “1,000 year reign” of Messiah on the earth as if it were the so-called “Church age”. He confessed that formerly he had been a “Pre-Millenialist” but had changed his position.

Augustine prevailed in his confrontation with Pelagius and his position has become the accepted doctrine of the Church. This position is obviously much more extreme than that taught by Jesus and the early Church, yet, it is the position embraced by virtually the whole Church. Indeed, Augustine defined “orthodoxy” in the Christian sense.

6. THIS GOSPEL OF THE KINGDOM

After considering the development of key Christian doctrines by the early Church fathers, we must now consider a basic change of the most fundamental vision of the Church. The message of the Church was changed in order to facilitate its needs. The message taught and preached by Jesus and the apostles after him was set aside and "another gospel" was emphasized. This "other gospel" is universally received today as the orthodox Christian message.

The Kingdom of God

The message of Jesus was the "Kingdom of God". He declared that He had been sent to preach this message,

> "But He said to them, 'I must preach the kingdom of God to the other cities also, For I was sent for this purpose'".[1]

As we consider the gospel account and the Biblical foundation on which it is based, we can formulate some cardinal points of this message. These include the teaching that:

> (1) God is establishing His direct rule or government in the earth, and this government will be manifested through Messiah;[2]
>
> (2) God will establish peace and judge (rule) the earth in righteousness;[3]
>
> (3) God will hold every man accountable for the

---

[1]Luke 4:43
[2]Psalms 2
[3]Psalms 98:9

deeds of this life;[4]

(4) He will introduce a period of "restitution of all things",[5] that will ultimately result in the removal of the curse on mankind;[6] and finally,

(5) The Messiah will return in the Glory of God.[7] As He does, God's Glory will reside in Jerusalem in a way similar to the phenomenon which occurred in the wilderness as Israel came out of Egypt.[8]

Some implications of these foundational points concerning the establishing of God's kingdom include:

(1) Every form of human government (international, national, state and local) will be abolished. Every constitution written will be voided because the government will "rest on His shoulders".[9]

(2) Human self-determination will end. "Every knee will bow, of those who are in heaven, and on earth, and under the earth, and that every tongue should confess that Jesus Christ is Lord, to the glory of God the Father".[10]

(3) The false dreams and illusions of man will be extinguished completely. God is the God of reality.[11]

---

[4]Ezekiel 18:4
[5]Acts 3:21
[6]Revelation 22:3
[7]Matthew 16:27
[8]Isaiah 4:5
[9]Isaiah 9:6
[10]Philippians 2:10-11
[11]Jeremiah 10:10

(4) Israel will be the only national entity that survives in the Kingdom. As God's elect nation, it will be exalted high above all the nations for praise, fame and glory.[12]

Jesus taught continually by parables to convey the basic message of the Kingdom. Prior to the time of Jesus, the Kingdom of God was envisioned as God's reign in Israel in the manner that occurred during the first Temple era. God was manifested during this era through His indwelling glory in the Temple and through His anointed prophets, priests and kings. Jesus introduced a new perspective of the Kingdom of God and began to lay the foundation for the establishment of this Kingdom during His earthly ministry. It would take millennia for its complete realization.

God would rule directly through the indwelling Holy Spirit in the hearts of believers. This was the fulfillment of the prophecy spoken by Ezekiel that God would:

> "Moreover, I will give you a new heart and put a new spirit within you; and I will remove the heart of stone from your flesh and give you a heart of flesh. And I will put My Spirit within you and cause you to walk in My statues, and you will be careful to observe My ordinances."[13]

Jesus also introduced the concept of the "*Living Temple*". His body was the temple during His earthly ministry. After His ascension the Church would function in this capacity. Ultimately this "Living Temple" would be established in Jerusalem just like the first Temple had been. As a "living stone" of this temple the individual believer was positioned or seated in the presence of the Living God.

As Jesus taught the principles of the Kingdom of God to His disciples, He used the *parable of the sower* to illustrate that the Kingdom of God was like the seed sown by a farmer,

---

[12]Deuteronomy 26:19
[13]Ezekiel 36:26-27

some falling on the roadway, some in thin soil, some in the midst of weeds and some on good ground.[14] He compared the conflict between the Kingdom of God and the kingdom of the world in the *parable of the wheat and the tares.*[15] The gradual growth of the Kingdom was explained in the *parable of the mustard seed* and the *parable of the leaven.*[16] The mysterious development was revealed in the *parable of growing grain.*[17] The practical function of the Kingdom of God in this age was revealed in the *parable of the dragnet.*[18] Again by means of a parable, Jesus taught that leadership in the Kingdom would be taken away from the natural leaders and would be given to those whose hearts were given to God.[19] Indeed, those least expected would be invited to participate in the Kingdom.[20] The opportunity for individual believers to function in the Kingdom was revealed in the *parable of the talents.*[21] The significance of the Kingdom to the individual believer was revealed in the *parable of the hidden treasure*[22] and the *parable of the fine pearl.*[23] Yet, vigilance would be required by those participating.[24] The Kingdom, God's direct rule, was not to be found externally established but would be accomplished by God's indwelling presence.[25] Finally, the amazing equality of reward, signifying eternal life in the presence of God, was shown by Jesus in the *parable of the workers.*[26]

These aspects of the Kingdom of God were introduced by Jesus and began being fulfilled through the early Church; they

---

[14]Luke 8:4-15
[15]Matthew 13:24-30
[16]Luke 13:18-21
[17]Mark 4:26-29
[18]Matthew 13:47-50
[19]Matthew 21:33-46
[20]Matthew 22:1-14
[21]Luke 19:11-27
[22]Matthew 13:44
[23]Matthew 13:45-46
[24]Matthew 25:1-13
[25]Luke 17:21
[26]Matthew 20:1-16

have continued to be fulfilled for almost 2,000 years. The vision outlined by these parables will not be fully realized until Jesus returns and reigns in Jerusalem directly in the midst of Israel.

Another Gospel

Now today, when we consider the basic message of the Church, we hear something different from Jesus' message of the Kingdom of God. The Church message focuses on the reconciliation of individuals to God. Paul outlined this message in his second letter to the Corinthians.[27] Indeed, this is a valid message for the Church to share in the midst of the nations. Nevertheless, as is obvious from our discussion of Jesus' message, the message of reconciliation in no way encompasses the Kingdom message taught by Jesus. The Church has basically spiritualized the Kingdom message and focused on the message or vision of reconciliation, which has been fairly faithfully set forth in the nations. Every denominational group has emphasized different aspects of this message, yet it is fundamental to all branches of the Church.[28]

Evidently, the Church determined to de-emphasize Jesus' message and substituted the message of reconciliation in its place. There are a number of reasons for this. The message of reconciliation is a "good, positive" message causing little reproach to the one who proclaims it. The Kingdom message, on the other hand, is like a sword causing a polarization in those who hear.[29] The one proclaiming the Kingdom message must bear reproach.

A second reason why the Church de-emphasized the Kingdom message is that God's Kingdom, as preached by Jesus, is intimately linked with Israel and Jerusalem. The

---

[27]II Corinthians5:18-20

[28]Please see Windall Willis, *The Kingdom of God in the 20th Century Interpretation*, Hendrickson Publishers, Peabody, MA, 1987.

[29]Matthew 10:34

Church succumbed to the pressure to adopt a universal identity while rejecting identity with Israel. Therefore, Jesus' message became awkward for them. The message of reconciliation, on the other hand, was easily adapted to the universal identity.

A final reason why the message of reconciliation was emphasized so strongly by the Church is that it was in the process of forming a new world religion -- Christianity -- distinct from that which preceded it. Like all religions it mapped out a way to come to God. The message of reconciliation served this purpose very well. The Kingdom message was unprofitable in the formation of this new religion.

There are probably any number of other factors that influenced this transition, but these three should be sufficient to outline for us why the message of reconciliation was emphasized at the expense of the Kingdom message. Today, this whole sequence is simplified in the minds of Christians by the rationalization that the message of Paul is the highest form of revelation available to us. They proclaim that Jesus preached His message to Israel, who they claim rejected it; therefore, God anointed Paul to bring forth this new universal message. Hence, the Church vision is logically built on Paul's message or letters rather than on the message of Jesus.

Today, as God has re-established the people of Israel in the Land of Israel, the Kingdom message is being preached again with a fresh anointing. With end time events rapidly being fulfilled, we are beginning to focus on the King and His message of the Kingdom. Indeed, this in itself is a sign of the end. Jesus proclaimed,

> "This gospel of the Kingdom shall be preached
> in the whole world for a witness to all nations,
> and then the end shall come".[30]

Jesus was not speaking of the "gospel of reconciliation", which has been set forth by the Church for almost two

---

[30]Matthew 24:14

millennia. He was speaking of the message of the Kingdom of God. The message of reconciliation could be preached to every living soul and we would not necessarily be nearer the goal of seeing the kingdom established. It is the message of the Kingdom that must be proclaimed.

7. A NATIONAL OR A UNIVERSAL PEOPLE?

Previously, we have outlined the historical separation that occurred between the Church and Israel. We considered a number of specific positions that were taken by the Church to distinguish itself from Israel. Now we will investigate the nature of God's people in the world. Did God intend to establish a national people separated from the world, or does He want a universal people without specific national identity? To answer this question, we will consider the positions of Israel and the Church.

Israel, A National People

From the very beginning, God separated the people of Israel from the rest of the nations. He called them to be *a goy kadosh*, a holy nation, and an *am segulah* or a peculiar people,

> "Now then, if you will indeed obey My voice and keep My covenant, then you shall be My own possession among all the peoples, for all the earth is Mine: and you shall be to Me a kingdom of priests and a holy nation".[1]

He said that He would set Israel "high above the nations",

> "And that He shall set you high above all nations which He has made, for praise, fame, and honor; and that you shall be a consecrated people to the Lord your God, as He has spoken".[2]

God gave this people a very specific land that further distinguished them. He honored Israel by dwelling in their midst and struck fear in the hearts of the nations by doing so. Even the Gentile prophet, Balaam, called Israel a people that

---

[1] Exodus 19:5-6a

[2] Deuteronomy 26:19

dwells apart,

> "As I see him from the top of the rocks, and I look at him from the hills; behold, a people who dwells apart, and shall not be reckoned among the nations".[3]

God dealt with Israel as a nation. Israel had one anointed leader and one altar. They shared a common experience of worship at the place God chose to establish His name. Israel stood before God as one people to seek atonement for the nation on Yom Kippur. Moses related God's message of blessings and curses to the people and they experienced them together. Israel was dispersed as a nation (586 BC) and has in this century experienced a regathering as a nation.

Israel was further distinguished by the Shabbat, which is a special covenantal sign between God and His people,

> "So the sons of Israel shall observe the sabbath, to celebrate the sabbath throughout their generations as a perpetual covenant. It is a sign between Me and the sons of Israel forever; for in six days the Lord made heaven and earth, but on the seventh day He ceased from labor, and was refreshed".[4]

Israel uniquely worshiped God during the festivals of the Lord (Passover, Shavuot and Sukkot). Israel alone had the opportunity and responsibility of Torah. Even the name of God by which He declared that He would be known to all generations, "*the God of Abraham, the God of Isaac, the God of Jacob*"[5] points to the patriarchs and, hence, to the nation of Israel. Therefore, we must conclude that God explicitly determined to sanctify (separate) His people Israel from all other nations; indeed, He required them to maintain that separation. Israel would have to deny its covenant, its Torah, its history and its future in order to be an ordinary nation like

---

[3]Numbers 23:9
[4]Exodus 31:16-17
[5]Exodus 3:14-15

all other nations.

The Church and Universal Identity

We have already documented the trend in the early Church toward a universal identity. The Church was strongly motivated to distinguish itself from Israel. It changed its day of worship to the first day of the week instead of the Biblical Shabbat. It developed new festivals in place of the Biblical festivals. It defined God by extra-Biblical philosophy. It established altars in each locality (in each church). It denied responsibility to the Torah, or Law, and redefined its primary vision from that of being a dragnet that draws the nations into accountability before the Lord to being an Ark of Safety in which people could escape the judgments of God.

The Church, in this way, denied its national character and became universal. Walker in his *History of the Christian Church* states that the Church saw itself as the "true Israel" whose citizenship was in the heavenly Jerusalem.[6] Walker further states that the conception of the Church was "of a heavenly citizenship reaching down to the earth, gathering into its own embrace the scattered Christian communities". Thus, today we hear people speaking of the universal, invisible Church. Its realm is heavenly and thereby encompasses all nations. It has no specific national character at all; it is truly catholic.

The Church's Role in Israel

At Mt. Sinai, Israel asked for an intermediary between themselves and God. Moses fulfilled that role. Following Moses came a sequence of judges and prophets. Each fulfilled the specific role of being the vessel of spontaneous

---

[6]Walker, *A History of the Christian Church*, pg. 38

anointing within Israel. After the era of the prophets, we see the complete office of Moses (prophet, priest and king) fulfilled in Messiah Jesus. Specifically, we see the vessel of God's spontaneous anointing in Him. After Jesus' ascension, that same anointing came upon the early Church. The role of the Church is identical to that of Messiah Jesus Himself. John proclaimed,

> "As He is, so also are we in this world".[7]

Paraphrasing Paul's message to the Romans he indicated that the role of Messiah was to confirm to Israel that every Biblical promise to her would be completely fulfilled.[8]

In order for the Church to function in this capacity and fulfill this ministry, it must be grafted into the national life of Israel. Paul contrasted believers before and after their life in Messiah including participation in the commonwealth (national life) of Israel,

> "Remember that you were at that time separate from Christ, excluded from the commonwealth of Israel, and strangers to the covenants of promise, having no hope and without God in the world".[9]

The clear implication of Paul's statement is that believers should now be considered to be included in the national life of Israel. Paul exhorted the Romans to remember that they had been grafted into the rich olive tree.[10] In other words, the Church must be identified with the nation of Israel if it is to serve Israel as a vessel of anointing. Obviously, at some point in the history of the Church, it faced the choice of maintaining a Biblical position of identity with Israel and the resulting national identity that goes with that position or adopting a universal (catholic) identity and message without a specific national identity. It is evident that by the second century the

---

[7] I John 4:17b
[8] Romans 15:8
[9] Ephesians 2:12
[10] Romans 11

latter choice was made.

Challenge

Today Israel is being regathered into the Land. At the same time, we see the nations moving into positions alarmingly like those predicted in the books of Daniel and Revelation. We are entering a time which demands that we search the Scriptures and our souls to ensure that we understand the will of God. As we do this, we discover that the Church has isolated itself from fruitfulness alongside of Israel through its universal identity. No ministry to Israel is possible as long as that universal identity is maintained. Just at the time when it appears that all the nations are being aroused to come up against Judah and Jerusalem, just when ministry could be most effective, the Church, in general, is not in a ministry position. In fact, it is completely isolated from Israel and is, therefore, incapable of effective ministry to Israel. What will the Church have to do in order to accomplish God's will in this day? It must humble itself, renounce universal identity and embrace the fact that it is a sub-group of Israel. The Church must realize that it is a special unit called and equipped to provide a unique and very special ministry to Israel in this day. This is especially true as Israel takes a more Biblical position and, hence, becomes more and more isolated in the midst of hostile nations.

God is raising up a church today that is identified with Israel. The Church is beginning to assume its true Biblical (national) identity within Israel, and to function in its true God-given capacity. Contrasted to this are many who rigidly maintain their catholic identity, refusing any identity with Israel. In the end, these will be open to identify with the great beast of the book of Revelation which will also be universal (catholic) in character. Today is the day to repent and come back to the "Hebraic roots" of our faith.

8. REDEMPTIVE ACTIVITIES AT THE CLIMAX OF THE AGE

In order to understand the role of God's people in His purpose today, we will consider the focus of His outworking throughout the ages. History can be divided into four distinct ages:

(1)	the Patriarchal Age	> 1400 BC
(2)	the Early Kingdom Age	1400 BC - 586 BC
(3)	the Age of the Gentiles	586 BC - 1967 AD
(4)	the New Kingdom Age	1967 AD >

The focus of God's outworking is somewhat different in each period. During the Patriarchal Age, God laid the foundation of redemption through the covenants and the revelation to the patriarchs. God's interaction with the nation Israel and His revelation through the prophets characterized the Early Kingdom Age. Throughout this period, God's attention was almost exclusively focused on the people of Israel. During the Age of the Gentiles, God's focus turned outward toward the nations. He dispersed Israel throughout the nations where they took a message of God's wrath,

> "A clamor has come to the end of the earth, because the Lord has a controversy with the nations. He is entering into judgment with all flesh; as for the wicked, He has given them to the sword, declares the Lord".[1]

Later, He dispersed the Church into the nations also. The Church conveyed the message of individual redemption,

> "Now all these things are from God, who reconciled us to Himself through Christ, and gave us the ministry of reconciliation, namely, that God

---

[1] Jeremiah 25:31

was in Christ reconciling the world to Himself, not counting their trespasses against them, and He has committed to us the word of reconciliation".[2]

So, during the Age of the Gentiles, Israel was used to bring a solemn warning of coming judgment to the national entities, while the Church preached individual reconciliation to the people of these same nations. Finally, during the New Kingdom Age, we expect God to prepare the way for and, indeed, establish His Kingdom through His Messiah.

The Beginning of a New Era

According to the ancient Hebrew prophets, we would expect that God would regather His people, Israel, to their land and that the focus of His attention would return to them in preparation for a new "Kingdom" age. Many believe this has been happening in the twentieth century. The Psalmist declared that God's attention and favor would return to Zion,

"For the Lord has built up Zion, He has appeared in His glory".[3]

Certainly, we can see that Zion is being built up today.

In addition, the prophets point to another activity of the Lord associated with the regathering of Israel; this is the judgment of the nations. Joel proclaimed that God would call the nations down into the valley of judgment when He restored the fortunes of Judah and Jerusalem,

"I will gather all the nations, and bring them down to the valley of Jehoshaphat. Then I will enter into judgment with them there on behalf of my people and My inheritance, Israel, whom they have scattered among the nations; and they

---

[2]II Corinthians 5:18-19
[3]Psalms 102:16

> have divided up My land".[4]

Zechariah foresaw the same thing happening in the last days,

> "Behold, I am going to make Jerusalem a cup that causes reeling to all the peoples around; and when the siege is against Jerusalem, it will also be against Judah. And it will come about in that day that I will make Jerusalem a heavy stone for all the peoples; all who lift it will be severely injured. And all the nations of the earth will be gathered against it".[5]

So we conclude that the regathering of the Jewish people and the establishment of the state of Israel initiated the promised judgment of the nations by God.

The Dragnet

Believers need to understand how to function in this new move of God. Jesus taught the message of the Kingdom of God. The explicit impact of the Kingdom is revealed in the parable of the dragnet,

> "Again, the kingdom of heaven is like a dragnet cast into the sea, and gathering fish of every kind; and when it was filled, they drew it up on the beach; and they sat down, and gathered the good fish into containers, but the bad they threw away. So it will be at the end of the age; the angels shall come forth, and take out the wicked from among the righteous. And will cast them into the furnace of fire; there shall be weeping and gnashing of teeth".[6]

Here, the Kingdom is seen as a dragnet bringing the whole world down into judgment.

There are two components of God's dragnet. The first is

---

[4]Joel 3:2
[5]Zechariah 12:2-3
[6]Matthew 13:47-50

the nation of Israel. Ezekiel proclaimed that the Lord would be sanctified in the midst of Israel in such a way that the nations would recognize His awesomeness and His identity,

> "And I shall magnify Myself, sanctify Myself, and make Myself known in the sight of many nations; and they will know that I am the Lord".[7]

For this to take place, Israel must be regathered in the midst of the family of nations. This has occurred throughout the twentieth century culminating with Israel becoming strong enough to declare itself an independent nation in 1948. Then God revealed Himself acting on behalf of Israel. At no time in modern history has this been more apparent than in the Six-Day War of June 1967. God openly demonstrated that He is uniquely committed to His people Israel and that He is determined to preserve, favor and exalt Israel above every nation.[8] Today, the attention of the nations is focused on God's people Israel in the land of Israel.

The second component of God's dragnet is the Church. When we speak of the Church we are expressly speaking of those local bodies of believers that are obedient to Messiah Jesus and are fully grafted into Israel. (We are not speaking of church denominations because each denomination in its own way attempts to rival the physical manifestation of Israel itself. In this way each has become a counterfeit. *Only the local church can be grafted into Israel.*) God has established bodies of believers in every tribe, tongue, people and nation.[9]

Paul declared that one very important function of the Church is to wage "spiritual warfare",

> "For our struggle is not against flesh and blood, but against the rulers, against the powers, against the world forces of this darkness, against the spiritual forces of wickedness in the heavenly

---

[7]Ezekiel 38:23
[8]Deuteronomy 26:19
[9]Revelation 5:9

places".[10]

He further indicated that the local church should impress the wisdom of God upon the rulers and authorities in the heavenly places,

> "In order that the manifold wisdom of God might now be made known through the church to the rulers and the authorities in the heavenly places".[11]

These rulers and authorities are understood to be demonic powers manifested through the nations. God's wisdom is impressed upon these demonic powers as the local church proclaims God's purpose in the community. In this way, truth is manifested throughout the world. A clear interpretation of what God is doing in Israel and throughout the world should be continually proclaimed in the local community. The nature of the demonic powers functioning in the nations should likewise be set forth. When this is done, the demonic host have no place to hide; their power of deception is greatly limited because of the light of the Lord shining through the local church. Thus, Israel and a grid of local churches scattered across the world form a network or dragnet which, on the one hand, proclaims God's sovereignty over the nations and, on the other hand, continuously reveals the nature of the spiritual forces which are driving the nations to destruction.

Church Identity

Now in order for this dragnet to function, the local church must be clearly identified with Israel or, in the words of Paul, it must be grafted into the rich olive tree. The dragnet cannot function if the Church is seen as a separate entity from Israel.

There are a number of things that the local church must do if it is to be grafted into Israel. First, Israel is a national

---

[10]Ephesians 6:12
[11]Ephesians 3:10

entity, so to be grafted in, the Church must see itself in a national sense. Thus the Church must repent from an independent universal identity. Secondly, the local church must return to a Bible oriented faith. The Bible must replace Church tradition in defining practice. Shabbat must be honored as the Biblical day of rest. Biblical festivals must be implemented in the place of Christian festivals. A thorough study of God's law must be made and the Church must confess responsibility for those aspects of the Law that are applicable to it. The Church must use explicit Biblical terms to address God and His Messiah in the place of terms based on Greek philosophical thought. Finally, the Church must openly confess its identity with Israel. The Scriptures give us a beautiful prophetic view of this identity in the book of Ruth. Ruth's interactions with Naomi foreshadows the Church's ministry to Israel in the last days,

> "But Ruth said, 'Do not urge me to leave you or turn back from following you; for where you go, I will go, and where you lodge, I will lodge. Your people shall be my people, and your God, my God. Where you die, I will die, and there I will be buried. Thus may the Lord do to me, and worse, if anything but death parts you and me'".[12]

When these Biblical practices are implemented, the Church is prepared to become functional in God's great dragnet.

Prophetic Fulfillment in the Twentieth Century

The twentieth century was unlike any time in preceding history. Truly we believe that we live in the end time. Some of the factors that distinguish the twentieth century and also constitute fulfillment of Bible prophecy include:

(1) the rapid population growth,

---

[12]Ruth 1:16-17

(2) advances in transportation, communication and data management,
(3) the emergence of a one-world government and religion and
(4) the regathering of Israel.

Population

The twentieth century has presented population problems unlike anything that has ever occurred previously. At the close of the twentieth century, the population of the world was near 6 billion. Currently, the doubling time for world population is estimated to be 30 to 40 years. If the function of population is integrated relative to time over all of human history, the number arrived at is about 20 billion. Hence, of all the people who have every lived, somewhere between one-fourth to one-third are alive today. In 30 years that fraction will be approaching one-half. It took at least six millennia to reach a population of 1 billion; now a billion is being added every five to ten years.

The consequence of such population growth is that mankind is beginning to severely stress the ability of the earth to sustain him; this problem will intensify in the twenty-first century. Famines are common in many areas now and they will only increase. The impact of natural disasters is magnified simply because of the increasing density of human population. These problems will drive the nations of the world into joint efforts in attempting to deal with these problems. Therefore, we can expect something like a global governmental effort to save the environment and to control and distribute food in the near future.

Technological Advances

Perhaps the greatest observable changes in the twentieth century occurred in the areas of transportation, communication and data management. Up until near the beginning of the 20th century, man traveled much the same way as Abraham did four thousand years ago. Today, travel to any part of the world is almost instantaneous. Transportation is inexpensive enough so that the masses freely travel about the globe; whereas, in the past only the elite traveled extensively. Easy, abundant transport has also made it possible, for the first time, to place a large army anywhere in the world in a very short period of time. A few years ago, the U.S. placed half a million troops halfway around the world in a matter of a few months. They were readily supplied with everything they needed to pursue their objective.

Communications also radically changed in the twentieth century. In previous centuries, communications were carried by couriers from one point to the other. This often required weeks or months for delivery. Today, we enjoy virtually instantaneous communication to any point on the globe. We can direct dial an acquaintance in any country. We send and receive FAXES or e-mail messages instantly. We read news on the Internet from every major capital as it occurs.

The advent of the computer has likewise revolutionized data management. In previous generations accounting was accomplished by hand ledgers. Today, we can deal instantly with an almost infinite amount of data by the use of computers. Indeed, detailed files are kept on every person. There seems to be no end to the quantity of data that can be dealt with or the speed by which it is done.

All of these factors have prepared the way for a single global government in the earth. Again, these advances in the twentieth century made the prospect of a single global government possible for the first time since Alexander the Great. Today a one-world government that encompasses every nation is entirely possible due to advances that have been realized in transportation, communication and data management during the twentieth century.

Globalism

The twentieth century witnessed the growing concept of a

global village and the vision of a one-world government. Following World War I, the League of Nations was formed. This constituted a global government in a limited sense. Following World War II, the United Nations was formed. The plans for the U.N. were much more ambitious than those for the League of Nations, although those ambitions were delayed due to the forty year struggle between East and West. Now in the last decade of the twentieth century, there remains only one "super-power" to dominate policy. We expect to see the potency of the U.N. to increase at the expense of national sovereignty in the 21st century. This emerging global government is prophesied to rule over every nation,

> "And authority over every tribe and people and tongue and nation was given to him".[13]

We believe this will be the "Anti-Christ" government which ultimately will make war against Israel and all true believers in Messiah Jesus.

The prophecies of the book of Revelation also point to the arising of a global religious order. This organization is seen as being molded in the image of the "secular" beast government. This, most likely, refers to a united religious order formed as a representative body with delegates from all major religious sects. If this organization is patterned after the U.N., then we would expect to see a "General Assembly" made up of representatives from all participating religious groups which would discuss policies for and admit new members to the organization. In addition we would anticipate an executive committee (like the Security Council)which would maintain the real decision making power of the organization. According to prophecy, this organization will exercise the power to include or exclude individuals from participation in the whole "Anti-Christ" system.

Efforts to establish a "United Religions" organization patterned after the United Nations is already underway. This

---

[13]Revelation 13:7b

effort has not, to date, received much publicity; however, it is sure to in the near future.

Ingathering of the Exiles

Now the only other thing that is necessary for the end-times is the regathering of the people of Israel to the land of Israel. This, of course, also occurred in the twentieth century. The First Zionist Conference was held in Basel, Switzerland in 1897. Following this conference, there was a steady flow of "Aliyah" to the land of Israel. The Jewish population in the land grew steadily throughout the century. By 1948 Jewish strength was sufficient to declare the existence of an independent state. In 1967, Israelis were able to take the heartland of Israel including Jerusalem. The ingathering continues.

Estimates of Jewish Population at Various Times	
1920	84,000
1948	750,000
1967	2,400,000
1980	3,200,000
Present	5,000,000

Summary

We stand today at a strategic point in history; every sign of the end times is being fulfilled. It is in this day that believers are being called to function in an extraordinary way in God's purpose. The great polarization of mankind is occurring. God's dragnet is beginning to function. Great light is shining in the world. As more light shines forth, the polarization will increase.

God will continue to sanctify Himself in the midst of Israel. As He does so, local churches that are grafted into Israel will receive a fresh and powerful anointing which will be manifested as more power and light. People will either be drawn to this light or repelled from it[14]. The nations are being forged into a global union of the government of the "Anti-Christ". The opposition to Israel is already apparent. Soon God will bring all the nations into the *valley of decision*,

> "Let the nations be aroused and come up to the valley of Jehoshaphat, for there I will sit to judge all the surrounding nations. Put in the sickle, for the harvest is ripe. Come, tread, for the wine press is full; the vats overflow, for their wickedness is great. Multitudes, multitudes in the valley of decision. For the day of the Lord is near in the valley of decision".[15]

In order to be effective in this crucial hour, believers in local congregations must be thoroughly grafted into Israel. They must embrace "Hebraic roots".

---

[14]John 3:20-21
[15]Joel 3:12-14

Part Two:

Establishing Hebraic Roots in the Local Church

1. INTRODUCTION

In the preceding section of this text, we discussed several concepts dealing with the history of the Church and Israel. We also considered a prophetic analysis of the situation that we find ourselves in today. In this final section we will discuss practical ways for a local congregation to begin establishing Hebraic roots.

We may begin by attempting to envision what the first century Church was like. We will discover that it is practically impossible to recapture the exact structure and atmosphere of that period. We can, however, build local churches which share the same fundamental characteristics with that early Church. Some of those foundational characteristics include, (1) *knowing God and His Messiah*, (2) *body faith*, (3) *Biblically sound vision and doctrine*, (4) *spiritual worship* and (5) *Hebraic identity*. Hebraic roots are not achieved by superficially embracing Jewish symbolism such as the wearing of kippot and talliot, reciting Hebraic liturgy and singing Hebrew songs. These things may be meaningful in certain circumstances but do not by themselves constitute "Hebraic roots". In this section we will consider how to build local churches with Hebraic roots.

It is the local church upon which we must focus our attention. An individual may embrace Hebraic roots to the point of formal conversion but he will not accomplish the goals set forth in this work. On the other hand, denominations due to their nature cannot adopt Hebraic roots. In fact, denominations are organized entities comprised of many local churches with a distinct physical manifestation in the world. These visible organizations invariably rival Israel. It is the local church that has the unique capacity to be the physical manifestation of Messiah Jesus in the world and, therefore, it is the local church which may properly adopt "Hebraic roots".

The Greek word for church is *Ekklesia*. It means simply "a calling out" or a group of people called out to a special assembly. The Hebrew word is *Knesset*. The twelve disciples of Jesus made up the first Church.[1] After Jesus' ascension the Holy Spirit came upon these same disciples and others like them forming a unique body of people in Jerusalem who were set aside by revelation knowledge of Messiah Jesus. These believers began to function as the Church. This church was centered in Jerusalem. It was made up of people from Jewish backgrounds. It functioned in the midst of Israel and was a part of Israel. It had Hebraic roots.

---

[1]Matthew 16:17

2. THE BEN-DAVID COVENANT

The Biblical foundation for the Church is found in the "*Ben-David*" covenant.[1] God made a covenant with the "son" of David promising Him a *kingdom*, a *throne* and a *house* forever. There was a short term fulfillment of this covenant in Solomon. The long term fulfillment came through Messiah Jesus. The angel announcing the conception of Jesus said,

> "And behold you will conceive in your womb, and bear a son, and you shall name Him Jesus. He will be great, and will be called the Son of the Most High; and the Lord God will give Him the throne of His Father David; and He will reign over the house of Jacob forever; and His kingdom will have no end".[2]

Jesus introduced the concept of the "Kingdom of God" during His earthly ministry. That kingdom was initiated in the early Church and will be fully and visibly manifested at His coming. This is the promised *kingdom*. After His resurrection, Jesus ascended into heaven and took His position at the right hand of the Father.[3] When He descends again His throne will be established in Jerusalem. This is the *throne* of David. Finally, Jesus referred to His physical body as the "Temple".[4] After the Holy Spirit fell upon the Church, the Church was referred to as the Temple. This, then, is the *house* God is building for David. Therefore, we see a complete fulfillment of the "*Ben-David*" covenant (*kingdom*, *throne* and *house*) through Messiah Jesus.

---

[1]II Samuel 7:8-17
[2]Luke 1:31-33
[3]Colossians 3:1
[4]John 2:21

3. FUNCTION OF THE LOCAL CHURCH

There are various functions of the Church. It has a primary responsibility to the house of Israel. Paul wrote that,

> "Messiah has become a servant to the circumcision on behalf of the truth of God to confirm the promises given to the fathers".[1]

Paul used the term *circumcision* in order to avoid any possible confusion. He, of course, is referring to the physical seed of Israel; those still distinguished by the circumcision. He recognized that the physical seed of Israel would continue throughout the generations and that all aspects of the covenants and all promises envisioned by the prophets would be fulfilled through them. He clearly stated that those called out in the Church bear a special responsibility to the people of the circumcision to confirm the truth of God. Most churches today deny this responsibility altogether. Many even hold the unscriptural position that Israel is no longer a legitimate covenant body in God's sight.

A second focus of ministry is to the nations. Again Paul wrote,

> "He has committed to us the word of reconciliation".[2]

The Church has a responsibility to convey to the people of the nations that God, the Holy One of Israel, has provided a blood covering for their sins and that they have been made acceptable in His presence. Therefore, men of all nations are called to repent from heathen lifestyles and to walk in uprightness according to the revelation of the one true God.

A third function of the local church is to serve the individual who has come to know Jesus as savior and lord. Jesus specifically charged His disciples to go into the nations and

---

[1]Romans 15:8
[2]II Corinthians 5:19

make disciples,

> "And Jesus came up and spoke to them, saying, 'All authority has been given to Me in heaven and on earth. Go therefore and make disciples of all the nations, baptizing them in the name of the Father and the Son and the Holy Spirit, teaching them to observe all that I commanded you; and lo, I am with you always, even to the end of the age'".[3]

The Church should serve as a place of development so the individual can grow in all aspects of godliness and righteousness. As one grows, the local church becomes a suitable vessel within which a sacrifice of service may be presented to the Lord on a daily basis.[4]

Finally, the local church is an instrument of spiritual warfare. Paul wrote,

> "For our struggle is not against flesh and blood, but against the rulers, against the powers, against the world forces of this darkness, against the spiritual forces of wickedness in the heavenly places".[5]

Here Paul outlined the arena of struggle that the Church has been commissioned for. The specific function of the Church is to speak truth under authority,

> "In order that the manifold wisdom of God might now be made known through the church to the rulers and the authorities in the heavenly places".[6]

So the Lord has convened local churches in every locality across the world and through them He challenges every principality. He will make known through the Church "the

---

[3]Matthew 28:18-20
[4]Romans 12:1
[5]Ephesians 6:12
[6]Ephesians 3:10

manifold wisdom [multifaceted purposes] of God" to the authorities in the heavenly places. These authorities are understood to mean demonic powers. In this present age the nature of this warfare is shining divine light on the activities of these authorities. Jesus will exercise a more forceful program at His coming.

4. THE FORMATION OF THE LOCAL CHURCH

It seems that two things are needed to form a new local church. First, a called minister, usually one functioning as an apostle, is sent forth with authority from Jesus to establish a new local church. Second, in the local community, other believers, in obedience to the Holy Spirit, are called together to form a local body with the called minister. This is a fulfillment of the words of Jesus,

> "Where two or three have gathered in my name,
> there I am in their midst".[1]

The tense of the Greek verb *gathered* is passive indicating that those gathered are convened by an outside agency. That agency, of course, is Jesus, Himself. Thus we may conclude that local churches should never be established by organizations but uniquely by called ministers who can boldly proclaim that they have been set aside by Jesus, Himself, to initiate such a work. This must be confirmed by a minimum of two or three others who confess by faith revelation that they are being called to form such a body. In such a setting, Jesus promises to be present.

Each local congregation (*ekklesia*) so formed has the unique capacity to manifest the very essence of the Messiah. A reproduction of the ministry of Messiah is effected in every locality in which it pleases God to establish a witness. We know from Scripture that such groups have been or will be established in every nation before God brings in the next phase of redemption.

> "And this gospel of the kingdom shall be preached in the whole world for a witness to all the nations, and then the end shall come".[2]

---

[1]Matthew 18:20
[2]Matthew 24:14

Role of the Pastor

The role of the pastor in the Church is to insure that Jesus is Lord of the congregation. He must not be lord himself, and must insure that no one else is. Obviously there are many other functions of the pastor in the local church. We want to concentrate on those duties which are necessary in establishing body faith.

Jesus becomes Lord by faith. There must be an interaction between Jesus and the Church resulting in specific direction for the congregation. The congregation must believe and obey. This constitutes body faith. Church government must be structured in such a way to implement and guard the process necessary for body faith.

In the past, church elders commanded enough respect that body faith could perhaps be based on their word. This is not true today. There seems to be little possibility today of body faith occurring based on anything less than full participation of the whole local body. Perhaps this has always been the case.

Only the pastor can establish and guard this type of procedure. He must carefully guide the congregation to consider any relevant issue under consideration. He must help define issues until everyone clearly understands what is being considered. Then he must lead the congregation in fasting and praying concerning the issue until the body arrives at the position of belief that they have (1) humbled themselves before the Lord, (2) interacted with the Lord concerning the given issue and have understood His direction and (3) believed and implemented His command. This is a tedious process. The pastor must work hard to insure that all are included; yet, at the same time, guard against manipulating the congregation into the position that he believes they ought to be. Any pastoral manipulation is deadly to the process of making Jesus Lord of the body. The typical political process employed in man's governmental efforts must be avoided. The Kingdom of God is a theocracy and Jesus is Lord. The entire government of the Church must "rest on His shoulders"[3]. Body faith is simply the means of making Jesus Lord of the Church.

Throughout history, Church leaders have employed all kinds of techniques in establishing church government. Constantine was probably most influential in establishing church councils as a means of governing all the churches across the empire. Since then, some leaders have led by intimidation. In other churches bodies of elders have made decision in back rooms and then exerted typical worldly, leadership techniques to implement their plans. Whatever the technique, the Church has operated on everything but body faith. Today body faith on the local church level is absolutely necessary for the congregation to establish "Hebraic roots".

Role of the Individual Member in Body Faith

We have discussed the role of the pastor in body faith; now we will consider the role of the individual church member in this process. The first essential step for the individual is to insure that he, personally, is supposed to be a part of the local body in question. This is a matter of *individual* faith not body faith. We maintain that every believer should be a part of a local church in order to serve the Lord in an orderly manner under God-established authority. However, the individual must determine which body he is supposed to be a part of. Pastors may invite believers to consider what a given church is doing but they should never attempt to get an individual or individuals to join the specific church that they are leading. It is Jesus' responsibility to assign individuals to the local church.

Once an individual determines that he is supposed to be a part of a given local church, he then is in a position to wholeheartedly join in the function of the body. It is the responsibility of the individual to seriously study issues that

---

[3]Isaiah 9:6

are under consideration by the body. He must honestly open himself before the Lord and seek understanding of the purpose of the Lord in the matter. He must join with others in fasting, praying and, therefore, participating in the process. When the body is called together to deal with the issue under consideration, he must participate with an open and expectant spirit and willingly join others in this process. Finally, as the body stands before the Lord, he must flow with the whole body in forming a consensus relative to the issue in question. Each must freely express what he or she believes the Lord is saying to them personally, yet, flow with the corresponding expressions of others. Usually, a consensus is gradually formed which integrates the wisdom of all. The important issue is that the whole body comes out of the experience with the belief that they have made Jesus Lord.

Faith Righteousness and the Local Church

There is a great deal of confusion concerning what constitutes the "righteousness of God". Many busy themselves today with what is accepted socially as righteousness. Some build churches, others engage in social ministries, while still others do prison ministries thinking that this is the work of God. In reality, the righteousness of God is initiated by revelation. Paul declared,

> "the righteousness of God is revealed from faith to faith".[4]

We can never determine the righteousness of God through philosophical deduction. Again, note the emphasis Paul gave to the fact that it is *revealed*. Jesus said that He only did what He saw His Father doing.[5] Again righteousness followed revelation as it always must. So for a local church or an individual disciple to accomplish God's righteousness, they must receive the direct revelation of what God wants to do

---

[4]Romans 1:17a
[5]John 5:19-20

and when He wants to do it.

Paul wrote,

> "For Christ is the end of the law for righteousness to everyone who believes".[6]

The Greek word translated "end" in this statement is *telos*. This word means "the goal or end attained". So Paul stated that Messiah Jesus was the goal for attaining righteousness. In other words, we as disciples should do exactly as He did. He heard from the Father and carried out what He heard. We should do likewise.

Another way of viewing this phenomenon is to recognize that we must *hear and obey* if we enter God's purpose. This is the faith process. The writer of Hebrews stated,

> "Now faith is the assurance of things hoped for, the conviction of things not seen".[7]

The things recorded in Scripture that reveal the plan and purpose of God are the basis of hope. The Holy Spirit adds assurance that God is working these things in us now. This then becomes faith. Therefore, hope is based on what God has done in the past; while faith is based on what God is doing now directly in our lives.

Faith in the Ministry of Messiah Jesus

Messiah Jesus is our *telos* or goal. The faith walk of Jesus is clearly seen in the gospels. We believe that He received two primary faith assignments from the Father during His earthly ministry. These assignments are particularly apparent in the gospel of Luke because Luke ordered the events of Jesus' ministry in chronological order. The first assignment was received during the period spent in the wilderness immediately following His baptism. Immediately following His experience in the wilderness, Jesus declared,

---

[6]Romans 10:4
[7]Hebrews 11:1

"I must preach the kingdom of God to the other cities also, for I was sent for this purpose".[8]

This is the dominant message preached by Jesus throughout His ministry.

The second assignment was received by Jesus at the "Mount of Transfiguration". Here Moses and Elijah spoke,

"Of His departure which He was about to accomplish at Jerusalem".[9]

Jesus came down from the mountain and steadfastly set His face to go to Jerusalem. Of course, this word of faith was completed as He died as the "Lamb of God" on the cross in Jerusalem.

These two primary missions define the earthly mission of Jesus. In both cases there was a period set aside to hear from God. There was a supernatural manifestation of God in both instances. Jesus heard a specific message which defined His mission. Therefore He could say, "I only do what I see My Father doing". The disciple should hear and obey in just this same way. The body of believers, the local church, should do exactly the same thing if it wishes to achieve "the righteousness of God'.

Faith and Body Life

Every aspect of our life should be founded on faith. Paul cautioned the disciples at Rome saying,

"Whatever is not from faith is sin".[10]

Obviously, a complete transition cannot be accomplished overnight. In reality, we "work out our salvation" little by little. As the Holy Spirit brings an area of our life under scrutiny, then we seek the Lord's will for it. In some areas the Lord will simply give us the freedom to decide for ourselves. Even in these cases we know we have actively submitted this particu-

---

[8]Luke 4:43
[9]Luke 9:31b
[10]Romans 14:23b

lar aspect of life to Him.

Body life should be governed in the same way. The body should fast and pray together until they have a revelation sense of the Lord's will for them. The mission of the Church should be determined in this way rather than following in the tradition of a given church or denomination. The whole body enters into the "righteousness of God" in this way.

Ministries to the Local Church

Jesus supplies certain specific ministries to each local church. These ministries were outlined by Paul as,

> "And He Himself gave some to be apostles, some prophets, some evangelists, and some pastors and teachers, for the equipping of the saints for the work of ministry, for the edifying of the body of Christ".[11]

These are often called the *five-fold ministry.* These ministries serve the local body of believers so they can grow up to the full maturity that is in Messiah Jesus. A minister has the responsibility to nurture individual believers in the manifestation of the gifts of the Holy Spirit rather than simply exercise the gifts himself. The very life of Messiah Jesus is manifested through the body of believers by the exercise of the gifts of the Holy Spirit. These gifts have been listed by Paul.[12] Jesus exercised all of these gifts with the possible exception of "tongues and interpretation of tongues". Each member should manifest at least one gift in order to function in the body. Manifestation of the gifts of the Holy Spirit can never be coerced but must be offered in faith by the individual believer.

---

[11]Ephesians 4:11-12
[12]I Corinthians 12:7-11

Gifts of the Holy Spirit

Paul outlined the operations of God the Father, Jesus the Messiah and the Holy Spirit. He said,

> "Now there are varieties of gifts, but the same Spirit. And there are varieties of ministries, and the same Lord. And there are varieties of effects, but the same God who works all things in all persons".[13]

We conclude that the Holy Spirit works through individuals who make up the local body of believers bringing forth specific manifestations through them. Also, each local body constitutes a distinct ministry and Jesus is the Lord of each local ministry. Finally, God the Father is ultimately responsible for all as He works various effects throughout the whole human community to accomplish His will.

The gifts of the Holy Spirit serve to reproduce the ministry of Messiah Jesus in a local setting. The most basic function of the local church is *to be the vessel of manifestation of Messiah Jesus*. He is the head of the Church which is His body. Since this is true, there must be an active functioning of the Holy Spirit in the body in order for Jesus to be seen. This alone should answer the question concerning the validity of the gifts of the Holy Spirit in the Church today. Each gift of the Holy Spirit brings forth one aspect of ministry that we see manifested in Jesus' earthly ministry. No individual brings forth all the gifts at any one time; therefore, it is necessary for each member of the body to be fruitful in the manifestations of the gifts.

Again, Paul lists the specific gifts as,

> "But to each one is given the manifestation of the Spirit for the common good. For to one is given the *word of wisdom* through the Spirit, and to another the *word of knowledge* according to the same Spirit; to another *faith* by the same Spirit, and to another *gifts of healing* by the one

---

[13] I Corinthians 12:4-6

> Spirit, and to another the *effecting of miracles*, and to another *prophecy*, and to another the *distinguishing of spirits*, to another *various kinds of tongues*, and to another the *interpretation of tongues*. But one and the same Spirit works all these things, distributing to each one individually just as He wills.[14]

As we study the earthly ministry of Messiah Jesus, we see the exact same manifestations through Him. Therefore, we conclude that the purpose of the gifts are to bring forth this extended ministry of Messiah Jesus through local bodies throughout the world.

- Jesus exercised the gift of *wisdom* when He was confronted by the religious leaders concerning paying taxes to Rome.[15] His answer shows supernatural wisdom which frustrated the schemes of the religious leaders who wanted to trick Him in taking a position for which they could make charges against Him.

- He exercised the gift of *knowledge* when He was speaking to the woman at the well in Samaria.[16] She perceived that He was a prophet because He exhibited supernatural knowledge.

- Jesus frequently exercised the gift of *faith*. He met Moses and Elijah on the Mount of Transfiguration. They spoke of His death which would occur in Jerusalem. He came down from the mountain and steadfastly set His face to go to Jerusalem.[17]

---

[14]I Corinthians 12:7-11
[15]Matthew 22:15-22
[16]John 4:7-19
[17]Luke 9:28-36, 51

- Jesus repeatedly exercised the gift of *healing*. When He was passing through Jericho on His way to Jerusalem, he healed the blind man.[18]

- Jesus accomplished *miracles*. When the disciples were in a boat and rowing across the Sea of Galilee, Jesus came to them walking on the water.[19]

- Jesus exercised the gift of *prophecy*. Just before He was crucified He prophesied concerning Jerusalem and the tribulations that would come upon it.[20]

- Finally, Jesus was able to *distinguish evil spirits* and exercise authority over them. He delivered a man who was controlled by a evil spirit when He was in the synagogue in Capernaum.[21] Many other examples could be cited from the ministry of Jesus.

The only gift of the Holy Spirit which does not appear to have been exercised by Messiah Jesus is the gift of *tongues*. It is possible that He worshiped God privately by the use of the gift of tongues; however, the Bible does not give us an account of it. The gift of tongues has both a private and a body function. Obviously, Jesus did not exercise this gift in the latter manner because there was no body (multi-member congregation) during His earthly ministry. The Church came into existence on *Yom Hashavuot* (The Day of Pentecost).

Each member of the body of Messiah should exercise at least one gift of the Holy Spirit. This is the only real way that the individual believer can be a functional part of the body. Many people exercise a number of different gifts. Paul exhorts

---

[18]Mark 10:46-52
[19]Mark 6:45-52
[20]Matthew 24:1-51
[21]Luke 4:31-37

us to seek spiritual gifts.[22]

Baptism of the Holy Spirit

How does a person become a part of the Church? Jesus said,

"You did not choose me, but I chose you".[23]

So we would say that the first step in entering the Kingdom of God is an invitation from the Lord. Assuming that by faith, we believe we have such an invitation, we must be "*born from above*"[24] in order to gain perception in the Kingdom. So the initiating experience is being "*born from above*" by the Holy Spirit or being baptized in and with the Holy Spirit. Jesus, the Messiah, is the one who "baptizes in the Holy Spirit".[25]

The concept of baptism is based on the practice of cleansing in the *Mikveh* practiced in Judaism. The Torah distinguishes between clean and unclean. Whenever someone became unclean, part of the process of becoming clean again involved the use of the mikveh. A person entering the mikveh totally immersed himself in the water. He was immersed, covered completely in the water. Therefore, the concept of "*Baptism in the Holy Spirit*" means that a person is immersed, covered or engulfed in the Holy Spirit.

Another way to consider the phenomena is that the Holy Spirit becomes an internal source of power and inspiration in the believer. God has loosed the Holy Spirit in the world today in a general sense. Jesus said that the Holy Spirit,

"When He comes, will convict the world concerning sin, and righteousness, and judgment".[26]

In contrast to the world, when an individual is baptized in the

---

[22] I Corinthians 14:1
[23] John 15:16
[24] John 3:3
[25] John 1:33
[26] John 16:8

Holy Spirit, the Spirit *begins* functioning from within the individual. Following the initial baptism the believer is exhorted to be continually filled with the Holy Spirit. So the Spirit indwells the individual on a continual basis and can, thereafter, be manifested through the individual. This is the means by which a person becomes potentially functional in the Church.

It is very important to understand that this baptism gives a person the capacity to perceive or see in the heavenly realm. Jesus said that,

> "Unless one is born again, he cannot see the kingdom of God".[27]

Paul added,

> "No one can say, 'Jesus is Lord,' except by the Holy Spirit".[28]

Beyond this, Paul taught that the Holy Spirit gives us the capacity to search out and understand even the depths of God. So it is the Holy Spirit that gives us the supernatural capacity to function in the Kingdom of God. There is no other way that a person can truly function in the local church except by the Holy Spirit.

What does a believer do to be "*baptized*" in the Holy Spirit? The first thing is to ask the Lord for it. We must ask and do so believing. Jesus said,

> "And I say to you, ask, and it shall be given to you; seek, and you shall find; knock, and it shall be opened to you. For everyone who asks, receives; and he who seeks, finds; and to him who knocks, it shall be opened. Now suppose one of you fathers is asked by his son for a fish; he will not give him a snake instead of a fish, will he? Or if he is asked for an egg, he will not give him a scorpion, will he? If you then, being evil, know how to give good gifts to your children, how much more shall your Heavenly Father give

---

[27]John 3:3b

[28]I Corinthians 12:3b

> the Holy Spirit to those who ask Him?".[29]

Secondly, we must believe that God desires us to have the Holy Spirit and will not deny our request. The writer of the book of Hebrews said,

> "And without faith it is impossible to please Him, for he who comes to God must believe that He is, and that He is a rewarder of those who seek Him".[30]

Finally, we must be willing to act on our belief. Without presumption, we must actively trust that God has granted our request. Many struggle needlessly at this point. However, God has granted that one specific manifestation of the Holy Spirit is given just to help us in this struggle. That gift is the "speaking in tongues". Paul said,

> "So then tongues are for a sign, not to those who believe[31] but to unbelievers".[32]

Tongues, or the use of a spiritual language, is a sign to us individually, as we are beginning to believe that we have indeed been baptized in or received the Holy Spirit. As we believe and exercise this gift, we are prepared to go on to the exercise of other gifts.

The most natural time to receive the Holy Spirit is in worship in the local church. Yet some readily believe and receive the desired baptism individually as they worship privately. Others need the support of the body worship. Still others need for the elders to lay hands on them in order to receive. It does not matter by which means we receive the Holy Spirit. The important thing is that we receive the Spirit and begin functioning in the body of Messiah. It is also important to understand that by the same pattern of belief by which we initially received the Holy Spirit, we are to be filled

---

[29]Luke 11:9-13

[30]Hebrews 11:6

[31]Those who believe are those already functional in the Church.

[32]I Corinthians 14:22a

daily. We can never take for granted that we are filled. We ask daily, we believe daily and we trust to be filled daily. The faithful disciple actively trusts God daily to continue to function in His purpose.

The Importance of Assembling with the Local Church

Each time the local body assembles, there is a unique opportunity for the resurrected Messiah to be manifested in great glory. Therefore, the writer of the book of Hebrews exhorted his readers saying,

> "Not forsaking our own assembling together, as is the habit of some, but encouraging one another, and all the more, as you see the day drawing near".[33]

It is vitally important that every member of the local body discipline himself to come together whenever the body is assembled in open worship. Obviously, there are times when a person is occupied and simply cannot come, but this should be the exception not the practice. Every effort should be made to join together with brothers and sisters. Whenever someone is absent the Holy Spirit is quenched to some degree. The more boldly the individual exercises the gifts in the body the more strongly his absence will be felt. Even if the individual does not boldly exercise the gifts, his presence alone is an encouragement to the body. Therefore, it is very important that we heed the exhortation of the writer of Hebrews.

In summary, God chose the mechanism of the local church to implement the ministry of the Messiah. The Church body is the body of Messiah. The Church should function under the delegated authority established by Jesus. The glorified Messiah is manifested through His body. Each member of the local church has been given gifts of the Holy Spirit. As the body comes together in worship, all the gifts

---

[33]Hebrews 10:25

added together reproduce the ministry of Messiah Jesus. In this manner, the ministry of Messiah Jesus is manifested in each society and in each age. It is important that each member has the faith to exercise the gifts imparted to him by the Holy Spirit. Likewise, it is important that each member come together with his brothers and sisters at each designated assembly. In this manner he becomes a source of encouragement to the whole body and the full vitality of the ministry of Jesus can be manifested through the local church.

5. WORSHIP AND HEARING

The most natural time for hearing from God is during worship. Worship in this sense is understood to be those times when believers open their hearts before the Lord in praise and adoration and allow the Holy Spirit to stir within bringing them to a real consciousness of standing in the presence of God. This can happen as the congregation of believers enters into worship. It can also happen to the individual in his private devotion before the Lord. In either case the living soul is supernaturally brought into the presence of God. It is at these times that the believer should learn to pray or ask concerning a specific mission of righteousness. The heart conviction that leads to faith flows out of the worship experience. This is one reason why Satan fights worship with such determination. If worship, whether body or individual, can be limited to ritual practice or intellectual thought, then no faith will be initiated.

The most basic characteristic of the "New Covenant" is that believers would all "know" God.[1] The root Hebrew word translated "know" is *yadah*. "Know" in this sense is as a man "knows" his wife, i.e., the term implies intimacy between the believer and God. The worship experience, whether individual or in the body, is therefore an experience of intimacy with God.

There are a number of conditions that must be met for a body of believers to enter into the worship experience. The local body of believers must be committed to the Lord and to one another. Unity based on love in Messiah is foundational to worship. In addition, the body must have attained to a reasonably holy walk in the Lord. Unholy living must be rooted out if the body is to worship. Beyond this, the body must humble itself before the Lord in order to be intimate with Him. Often today, congregations are stirred through music to a

---

[1]Jeremiah 31:34

triumphant high devoid of humility. There is no true Biblical worship in such events. Humility and the corresponding confession of dependance on the Being of God is a necessary prerequisite for worship. Finally, praise leads to true spiritual worship.

The local body of believers has a unique capacity to offer up spiritual sacrifices to God in Messiah Jesus. Peter declared,

> "You also, as living stones, are being built up as a spiritual house for a holy priesthood, to offer up spiritual sacrifices acceptable to God through Jesus Christ".[2]

The basic vision for worship is Jesus mystically arising in the body to offer up spiritual sacrifices to God. Jesus functions in the body through the gifts, or manifestations, of the Holy Spirit. Worship, therefore, is comprised of Jesus being manifested through the body by the Holy Spirit and interacting uniquely with the Holy One. In this way Jesus and His body *know* the Father. This is the significance of Jesus' statement,

> "Jesus said to him, 'I am the way, and the truth, and the life; no one comes to the Father, but through Me'".[3]

The Bible maintains that God is enthroned on the praises of His people.[4] Praise, therefore, along with humility is necessary for worship. Generally, songs of praise expressly directed to our Lord Jesus bring the body into a deepened unity and love as the Holy Spirit stirs within each individual. As praise continues, the reality of Messiah Jesus' presence becomes more and more evident in the hearts of the believers. Jesus said,

> "And this is eternal life, that they may know thee, the only true God, and Jesus Christ whom Thou

---

[2]I Peter 2:5
[3]John 14:6
[4]Psalms 22:3

> hast sent".[5]

Eternal life and worship are experienced both with the Holy One and with Messiah Jesus. Thus intimacy with Messiah Jesus generally precedes intimacy with the Holy One.

The ultimate focus of worship must be to the Holy One. We have an account recorded in the gospels of Jesus worshiping the Holy One.

> "At that very time He rejoiced greatly in the Holy Spirit, and said, I praise Thee, O Father, Lord of heaven and earth, that Thou didst hide these things from the wise and intelligent and didst reveal them to babes, Yes, Father, for thus it was well-pleasing in Thy sight".[6]

The vision of worship, therefore, is that Messiah Jesus, as He is mystically manifested in His body, rejoices and praises the Holy One in a manner like that recorded by Luke.

Hebraic worship then is intimacy with the Holy One and with the Messiah. Individually, the believer is equipped for intimacy with Messiah Jesus due to the Holy Spirit dwelling within. The local church, however, is the "body" of Messiah and in the body under Jesus' Lordship we may uniquely approach the Holy One.

The by-product of worship is salvation, deliverance and healing. The presence of God brings all of these effects in the life of the believer.

---

[5]John 17:3
[6]Luke 10:21

6. CHURCH IDENTITY

The most basic issue that must be dealt with in establishing "Hebraic roots" has to do with the identity of the local church. There are two basic identities that a church may assume. One is the traditional Christian identity of the universal catholic church. Catholic in this case means universal or non-national. The other possibility is an identity with Israel. These two camps are mutually exclusive. Each church must choose to fit within one or the other.

The Church of the second century deliberately chose to establish an identity separate from Israel. The Church came to be seen as an independent entity which was anchored in heaven but had a manifestation in the earth spreading across all nations. Hence, it was *catholic* or *universal*. This means specifically that it is not associated with any given national people and, in particular, it was not associated with Israel.

Since that time, the Church has maintained this universal identity. Therefore, Christianity evolved as a world religion without "Hebraic roots or identity". Every daughter church formed throughout the ages shared this catholic identity. The Baptist Church in this case is as catholic as the Roman Catholic Church. As discussed earlier, alternates to Biblical festivals were developed to maintain the separation from Israel. In addition, unscriptural doctrinal teachings were also developed which further widened the gap between the Church and Israel.

The alternative identity that a church may chose is with Israel. This is done by simply assuming a true Biblical identity. The first century Church certainly maintained such an identity. It was known as a sect of Judaism called "*The Way*". Israel must be seen as an elder brother rather than an alien enemy.

Establishing an identity with Israel does not imply any acceptance on the part of Israel. True Hebraic identity is a matter of faith and does not depend upon acceptance by anyone except by God Himself. Some struggle very hard for acceptance from Israel, yet, the anointed vessel in Israel was rarely accepted. Moses, Jeremiah and Jesus are notable examples of this phenomena. Neither was accepted during their lifetime. Due to the long history of conflict between the Church and Israel, it is wise to walk simply in faith and reach out in ministry to Israel. True Godly love and concern will result in the establishment of at least good will.

One danger exist in the area of identity. Believers sometime tend to become so "Jewish" that they become an affront to Israel. Hebraic roots is not obtained by mimicking Jewish ethnic traditions and customs. Believers must be careful to implement just those things which are clearly established in the Scriptures without making any assumptions about or demands on Israel. Too much Jewish tradition implemented without wisdom can lead to the attitude of being the "true Israel". This can become just another form of replacement theology. This can be seen today in some "Messianic Jewish" groups.

A local church does not need to renounce ties with the Christian community in order to establish "Hebraic roots". To the degree that other local churches are making Jesus their Lord, in real terms, a brotherhood exists that should be maintained. If there is a break between the local church that is establishing "Hebraic roots" and the Christian community, in general, let it be initiated by the community not by the local church.

7. SUMMARY

Any local body of believers can begin to seek for and establish Hebraic roots. The concepts discussed above should serve as a guide. The practical realization of body life, body faith and body worship is essential. These will not be discovered instantly, but, must be worked out over a period of time. The group of believers that sincerely seek such purpose and identity will surely be blessed by God.

Bibliography

Baker, Robert, *A Summary of Christian History*, Broadman, Nashville, 1959.

Boyle, Isaac, *A Historical View of the Council of Nice*, Baker Book House, Grand Rapids, Michigan, 1988.

Lochs, Samuel and Wachs, Saul, *Judaism* Argus Communications, Niles, Illinois, 1979.

Roberts, A and Donaldson, J., editors, *Ante-Nicene Fathers*, Hendrickson, Peabody, MA, 1994.

- Cyprian, *The Treaties of Cyprian*, Treatie VI.
- Cyprian, *Letters LI.*
- Epistle of Ignatius to the Ephesians.
- Epistle of Ignatius to the Magnesians.
- Epistle of Ignatius to the Smyrnaeans.
- Epistle of Polycarp to the Philippians.
- The First Epistle of Clement to the Corithians.
- Iranaeus, *Against Heresies.*
- Justin, *The Apology.*
- Justin, *Dialogue with Trypho.*
- Justin, *The First Apology.*
- Origen, *Against Celsus.*
- Origin, *De Prinapiis.*
- Tertullian, *AD Nationes.*
- Tertullian, *Against Praxeas.*
- Tertullian, *An Answer to the Jews.*
- Tertullian, *The Apology.*

Schaff, P, editor *Nicene and Post-Nicene Fathers*, Hendrickson, Peabody, MA, 1994.

- Augustine, *On The Trinity.*
- Augustine, *The City of God.*

Wagner, Clarence, *Covenants*, Bridges for Peace, Jerusalem, Israel.

Walker, Williston, *A History of the Christian Church*, Charles Scribner's Sons, NY,1970.

Wilson, Marvin, *Our Father Abraham*, William B. Eerdmans Company, Grand Rapids, MI and Center for Judaic-Christian Studies, Dayton, Ohio, 1989.

Index

Further Information

If you have questions regarding any of the subjects covered in this book, or if you desire to learn more about the implementation of the concepts put forth in this book, you may contact us at the following address:

Tzemach Institute for Biblical Studies
P.O. Box 181191
Casselberry, FL 32718

You may also contact us via email at:
ken@tzemach.org or *tzemach@tzemach.org*
Or visit our website at: *http://www.tzemach.org*

Other books by Kenneth Garrison:

God's Final Call?

Redemption

Bible Prophecy